TAKING POPULATION SERIOUSLY

Frances Moore Lappé
Rachel Schurman

A Food First Book
The Institute for Food and Development Policy
San Francisco

First published in 1988 by the Institute for Food and Development Policy as "The Missing Piece in the Population Puzzle," Food First Development Report No. 4, September 1988.

Printed in the United States of America
ISBN: 0-935028-53-6

Design: Constance King
Cover Design: Susan Galleymore
Typesetting: Access Typography
Printing: West Coast Print Center

FOOD FIRST

The Institute for Food and Development Policy (FOOD FIRST) is a nonprofit research and education center, which, since its founding in 1975, has been dedicated to identifying the root causes of hunger, poverty, and environmental degradation in the United States and around the world. Financed by thousands of members, with modest support from foundations and churches, FOOD FIRST speaks with a strong, independent voice, free of ideological formulas and vested interests.

In over 50 countries and 20 languages, FOOD FIRST provides a wide array of educational tools—books, articles, films, and curricula for elementary schools and high schools—to lay the groundwork for a more democratically run society that will meet the needs of all.

For more information about Food First publications, please write or call:
The Institute for Food and Development Policy
145 Ninth Street
San Francisco, CA 94103
(415) 864-8555

CONTENTS

ILLUSTRATIONS

Figures

Tables

ACKNOWLEDGMENTS

Our colleagues at the Institute for Food and Development Policy deserve our special thanks for their excellent counsel and careful assistance in the development of this analysis: Walden Bello, Medea Benjamin, Marilyn Borchardt, Becky Buell, Joseph Collins, Kevin Danaher, Andrea Freedman, Susan Gallymore, Audee Kochiyama-Holman, Marshall McComb, and Ann Kelly. We also appreciate the research assistance of Heidi Beirich and Michele Mattingly.

Many others with special knowledge in this field also provided valuable comments and criticism. Our special thanks go to Will Alexander, Leon Bouvier, John Caldwell, Ansley Coale, Phillips Cutright, Joel Dirlam, Joan Gussow, Betsy Hartmann, W. Parker Mauldin, Thomas Merrick, Alberto Palloni, John Ratcliffe, Robert Repetto, and Bernard Schurman. Of course our gratitude in no way suggests that our reviewers agree with our analysis.

ONE

THE POPULATION PUZZLE

FIGURE 1: Population Growth, 1750–2100

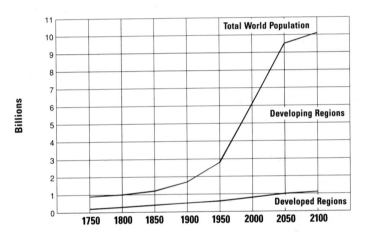

SOURCE: Thomas W. Merrick, "World Population in Transition," Population Bulletin, Vol. 41, No. 2 (Washington, D.C. Population Reference Bureau, Inc., reprinted January 1988)

What do you see in this picture?

If what you see is a population "explosion," you are not alone. That's precisely what biologist Paul Ehrlich dubbed these trends in his eye-opening 1968 book, *The Population Bomb*. Population growth rates in the third world are historically unprecedented. The world population has doubled since 1950, with 85 percent of that growth occurring in the third world.

But what set off the population bomb? What problems does it present? And how can we defuse it to help bring human population into balance with the natural environment? In the past twenty years, this graph of population trends has become almost a "Rorschach test" in which people have seen strikingly different answers to these critical questions.

In this report, we briefly critique several current interpretations of the population puzzle and point beyond them to an emerging alternative framework for understanding — one that incorporates unmistakable historical lessons.

We first consider the perspective of the biological determinists — those who see human populations overrunning the carrying capacities of their ecosystems. We suggest why this view has been largely discredited and describe a milder version that dominates public perceptions of the population problem today. In the latter view, the crux of the population crisis is that growing numbers of people are overwhelming finite resources; the answer is obvious — reduce births.

Over the last two decades a much more useful analysis has emerged among social scientists, replacing both of these narrow views. It describes the realities of poverty and premature death that keep birth rates high. While we incorporate many of its invaluable insights here, we must dig substantially deeper to seriously confront the population problem.

In this report we seek to probe beneath the descriptive social perspective in order to examine the relationships of social power — economic, political, cultural — that influence fertility. We construct what we call the *power-structures perspective*, referring to the multilayered arenas of decision-making power that shape people's reproductive choices or lack of them. We use this framework to show how the powerlessness of the poor often leaves them little option but large families. Indeed, high birth rates among the poor can best be understood, we argue, as a defensive response against structures of power that fail to provide, or actively block, sources of security beyond the family. From this perspective, rapid population growth is a *moral* crisis because it reflects the widespread denial of essential human rights to survival resources — land, food, jobs — and the means to prevent pregnancy.

It follows from our power-structures perspective that far-reaching economic and political change is necessary to reduce birth rates to replacement levels. Such change must enhance the power of the poorest members of society, removing their need to cope with economic insecurity by giving birth to many children. Social arrangements beyond the family — jobs, health care, old-age security, and education (especially for women) — must offer both security and opportunity. Most important, the power of women must be augmented through expanded opportunities for both men and women. At the same time, limiting births must become a viable option by making *safe and acceptable* birth control devices universally available.

In seeking solutions to the population problem, we examine critical lessons from the handful of third world countries that have been exceptionally successful in reducing fertility. In each, we find our thesis reinforced: far-reaching social changes have empowered people, especially women, and provided alternative sources of income, security, and status to child bearing.

Humanity ignores such lessons at great peril. Unless we are honestly willing to confront the roots of people's powerlessness, we cannot hope to halt population growth in the future — with dire consequences for human well-being and for the biosphere itself. But the consequences are immediate as well: unwillingness to address the social roots of high fertility leads almost inexorably, we argue, to coercive, even hazardous population control strategies, jeopardizing the goal of enhanced human well-being.

Moreover, lacking an approach that addresses the problem of social power, we can expect no relief to the misery of hunger and the stress of environmental decline, *regardless* of success in cutting birth rates.

Finally, we challenge everyone alarmed about rapid population growth to be fully concerned not just about its impact on humanity but on nonhuman life as well.

Learning the Population Lingo

Reading the population literature, it's easy to become confused by technical terms. We hope a simple explanation of some of the more commonly used terms can help.

Crude Birth Rates. The crude birth rate, or CBR, literally measures the number of live births for every thousand women. The CBR refers to a country as a whole or to a particular subgroup within a country. "Crude" refers to the fact that it does not take into account the age structure of a population, which greatly affects the number of births in any given year. For example, if two countries have the same number of people, but one has twice as many women of childbearing age, it will have a much higher crude birth rate. For this reason, the CBR is not directly comparable across countries, or even across time. It is often used by demographers when better measures are lacking.

Total Fertility Rates. This rate, often abbreviated as TFR, can be thought of as the average number of children that a woman will have over her reproductive lifetime. It is hypothetical in the sense that it does not represent the lifetime experience of any particular woman or group of women, but represents a composite measure. The TFR is calculated as the sum of birth rates specific to each age group of women and assumes that each cohort's fertility will hold during the lifetime of the "hypothetical woman."

Population Growth Rate. The population growth rate is the rate at which a particular population is growing each year. It is calculated relative to a base population size (say, the population size in the preceding year), and reflects the effects of births, deaths, and migration. The current growth rate in the United States is about 1.0 percent per year.

Replacement Level. A population that is at replacement level will exactly replace itself over the course of a generation with no growth and no decline. In the industrialized countries, replacement level usually corresponds to a TFR of 2.1; in other words, each woman would bear two children, one to replace herself and the other to replace her mate. (The additional .1 births is necessary to offset a small number of infant deaths and childless women.) In the third world, replacement levels are somewhat higher — about 2.5 — because of the higher infant death rates.

TWO

THE POPULATION DEBATE

What Set Off the Population Explosion?

The widely accepted explanation of what tripped the population wire in the third world is that a rapid drop in death rates occurred without a parallel drop in birth rates. With more people living longer, but as many babies still being born, populations began to grow fast.

While a similar shift was typical of the first stage of a transition to slow population growth in the now industrial countries, what has happened in the third world is different. The mortality decline there has been sharper than that which occurred in Western Europe and the United States, and it happened against a backdrop of higher initial birth rates.[1]

What accounts for this sharp drop in deaths? Here, demographers hardly agree. Some point to the introduction of vaccines, antibiotics, and pesticides from the industrial countries; others stress improvement in education, sanitation, and nutrition.

And why haven't birth rates declined, too? They have, but not nearly enough to prevent rapid population growth in most third world countries.

But don't be too alarmed, many population experts tell us. It is only a matter of time before a decline in birth rates will mimic the decline in death rates. The world's population will thus level off or plateau, they predict, about a century from now at about 10 billion, double the world's current population.[2]

We're not so sanguine. While death rates may be brought down, at least somewhat, by imported technologies or public health initiatives, birth rates are not so easily affected. They reflect intensely personal choices in response to a host of economic, social, and cultural forces. Until the forces underpinning high birth rates start to change, we doubt that it is possible to predict the timing of a human population plateau.

Some demographers share our concern. "Forget plateaus," says population specialist Phillips Cutright. Such projections are likely to be "wishful thinking," he warns.[3] And recent data confirm Cutright's skepticism. Global population is growing faster than expected because many of the most populous nations — China, India, Pakistan, Egypt, and Iran to name a few — are not following the expected pattern of a smooth and continuous fertility decline.[4]

Population: What's the Problem?

To make our own analysis most clear, let us begin with a brief outline of the main schools of thought concerning the nature of the population problem. We present three alternative perspectives and then our own.

More people — no problem perspective. To some, population growth is no threat at all. To the contrary, it may actually *contribute* to economic development and higher living standards.

Julian Simon, author of *The Ultimate Resource*, is perhaps the best-known advocate of this position. Writing in *Science*, Simon argues that in industrial countries, additional people stimulate higher productivity.[5] Growing populations in third world countries also "have a positive net effect on the general standard of living," apparent only in the long term.[6] Simon and his supporters marshal largely historical evidence. If improvements in technology and productivity have surpassed growth in population so far, why not indefinitely, they ask.

While Simon's view is not widely accepted, his influence can be easily detected in recent mainstream pronouncements on population. In 1986, a report by the National Academy of Sciences downplayed population as a problem, stating that "concern about the impact of rapid population growth on resource exhaustion has often been exaggerated."[7]

In our view, Simon's perspective must first be rejected on ethical grounds. It implies that the impact of population growth can be judged solely as to how it affects human well-being, ignoring any responsibility toward the integrity of the larger ecosphere. Second, its presumption that population growth isn't a problem because of infinite human ingenuity to discover replacements for any depleted resource is blind to the fact that the natural world is a delicate, interacting system, not merely an emporium of separate, replaceable parts. Simon fails to consider the possibility that our efforts to support ever larger numbers is destroying that delicate environmental balance. Because we reject this perspective's first premises, we do not examine it in depth.

People-versus-resources perspective. The much more widely held view, that which has shaped popular understanding since the 1960s, stands Simon's position on its head: people are pitted against finite resources and we're fast overrunning the earth's capacity to support us. In fact, current environmental degradation and hunger suggest that in some places we've already pushed beyond the earth's limits.

This conceptualization of the problem came vividly into popular consciousness with Paul Ehrlich's *The Population Bomb*, first published in 1968. Ehrlich convinced many people that fast-growing populations meant that we had reached the earth's limits to feed people. Ehrlich wrote:

> The battle to feed all of humanity is over. In the 1970's the world will undergo famines — hundreds of millions of people are going to starve to death in spite of the crash programs embarked upon now.[8]

In *Famine 1975!*, published the year before Ehrlich's book, William and Paul Paddock warned that catastrophe was imminent.[9]

By the 1980s, emphasis within the people-versus-resources perspective was less on the danger of humanity simply running out of land to feed itself than on the destruction of the environment by expanding populations. Ehrlich's underlying assumptions have continued to hold sway in the popular consciousness. Perhaps the most widely read expression of this view today comes from the Worldwatch Institute in Washington D.C. In a 1986 Worldwatch publication, Lester Brown and Jodi Jacobson describe the threat of continuing high rates of growth:

> Our contemporary world is being divided in two by demographic forces.... In the...half where birth rates remain high, rapid population growth is beginning to overwhelm local life-support systems...leading to ecological deterioration and declining living standards.[10]

According to Brown and Jacobson, in many third world countries, this process is already well under way.[11]

An extreme version of this perspective is found in the work of biologist Garrett Hardin. He takes the answer to the question "What is the population problem?" a further step toward strict biological determinism. As the influential economist Thomas Malthus argued in the early nineteenth century, Hardin claims that our biology drives us to reproduce at a rate faster than our resources can sustain. Without government policies to prevent it, we are destined to overrun our resource base, with hunger the tragic outcome.[12]

For Hardin, of immediate concern is not the threat of global food shortage, but population-caused food shortages at the national and local levels. In his view, the populations of some countries have already overrun their biological "carrying capacities." To

Hardin, Ethiopia's repeated famines clinch his case.[13] His views are now echoed by some hard-line environmentalists, like Earth First! founder Dave Foreman.

This extreme neo-Malthusian view is generally discredited. But a soft-pedaled version — still posing people against resources as the essential problem — captures considerable media attention and dominates the popular understanding of the problem today.

Much of our prior work, especially *Food First* and *World Hunger: Twelve Myths*, is a refutation of this still-influential resources-versus-people perspective. We demonstrate the illogic of seeing population as a root cause of hunger when in so many cases population density and hunger are not demonstrably related. China, for instance, has only half as much cropped land per person as India, yet Indians suffer widespread and severe hunger while the Chinese do not. Sri Lanka has only half the farmland per person of Bangladesh, yet when effective government policies kept food affordable, Sri Lankans were considerably better fed than Bangladeshis. Costa Rica, with less than half of Honduras' cropped acres per person, boasts a life expectancy — one indicator of nutrition — fourteen years longer than that of Honduras, and close to that of the industrial countries.[14] And Cuba, which leads the third world in life expectancy, low infant mortality rates, and good nutrition, has a population density similar to Mexico's, where hunger is rampant.

This lack of a clear link between population density and hunger (highlighted in table 1) is a strong rebuttal to the people-versus-resources conception of the problem. Many other factors beyond sheer numbers obviously determine whether people eat adequately; among them are whether or not people have access to land to grow food, or have jobs providing them with money to buy it.

The same simplistic formulation must be rejected when it comes to environmental destruction. An obvious example is the ecolog-

TABLE 1: Hunger and Population Density
(Acres of Cropland Per Person in 1980, Selected Countries*)

Population Density	Significant Hunger		Less Hunger	
High	Burundi	.070	Singapore	.007
	Bangladesh	.25	Japan	.10
	El Salvador	.37	So. Korea	.14
	Haiti	.38	China	.25
	Rwanda	.47	Israel	.26
			Mauritius	.28
			No. Korea	.31
			Sri Lanka	.36
Moderate	Philippines	.50	Venezuela	.54
	India	.60	Costa Rica	.54
	Guinea	.72	Malaysia	.76
	Mexico	.85	Cuba	.80
	Burkina Faso	.93		
	Thailand	.93		
	Nigeria	.97		
Low	Honduras	1.15	Hungary	1.23
	South Africa	1.17	Chile	1.24
	Brazil	1.24	Uruguay	1.61
	Afghanistan	1.28	United States	2.07
	Angola	1.29	Argentina	3.11
	Chad	1.68		

SOURCE: Adapted from Francis Urban and Thomas Vollrath, *Patterns and Trends in World Agricultural Land Use*, U.S. Department of Agriculture, Foreign Agricultural Economic Report no. 198, Washington D.C., 1984, table 2 (original data from the UN Food and Agriculture Organization).

*Cropland consists of arable land and land in permanent crops.

ical havoc now being wrought in the Brazilian Amazon. The slash-and-burn agriculture of Brazilian peasants often gets the blame. But if land in Brazil were not the monopoly of the few — with 2 percent of the landowners controlling 60 percent of the arable land — poor Brazilians would not be forced to settle in the Amazon, destroying the irreplaceable rain forest. And surely the logging and cattle ranching, also destroying rain forests, reflect not population pressure but market demand for meat and wood by better-off consumers, largely in the industrial countries.

The social perspective. Fortunately, over the past two decades, an outline has emerged of a strikingly different answer to the question, "What is the problem?" It draws on the research of scores of anthropologists, sociologists, and economists. This newer perspective has taken hold in such varied institutions as the World Resources Institute, the Population Reference Bureau, the UN Fund for Population Activities, and the World Bank. In the 1980s, some from the food-versus-resources perspective, including the Worldwatch Institute, have acknowledged the findings of the social scientists.

The social perspective takes a look beneath the threat of populations overrunning resources to ask *why* third world populations are growing so fast, pointing to a complex interaction of economic, social, and cultural forces that keeps third world fertility high. They include the low status of women, the high death rates of children, and the lack of old-age security.

This perspective presents a powerful challenge to the people-versus-resources view in which growing populations deplete per capita resources, leading to hunger and environmental degradation. In the social perspective it is the realities of poverty that lead to both rapid population growth and hunger. High fertility becomes an effect more than a cause of poverty and hunger.

The power-structures perspective. Building on the previous work of the Institute for Food and Development Policy, in this report we seek to synthesize crucial insights emerging from this social perspective, while pushing its analysis still further.

Peeling away another layer, we ask what lies behind the poverty and insecurity keeping birth rates high. In answering, we add a critical dimension without which we believe it is impossible to understand population patterns: *power*. By this we mean, very concretely, the relative ability of people to have a say in decisions that shape their lives, from those decisions made at the family level to those that are international in scope.

How society distributes power determines which human rights are acknowledged and protected. We find it most fruitful to view the varied forces keeping birth rates high as aspects of a systematic denial of essential human rights — understood to include not only political liberties, but access to life-sustaining resources and to educational and economic opportunity.

In our common search for solutions, we challenge all who are beginning to grasp the true social — rather than biological — roots of rapid population growth to follow through on the logical consequences of this deeper analysis. Unfortunately, it is in defining solutions that the promising social perspective falls flat. It describes the link between poverty and high fertility, but it fails to confront the forces that generate and perpetuate poverty.

The consequences are momentous. Ignoring the social roots of hunger while still trying to reduce birth rates leads almost inexorably to more coercive birth control technologies and programs that jeopardize people's health and self-determination.

Finally, we call for a shift in the entire debate about the population problem to incorporate insights emerging from environmentalists and from the land stewardship movement. Drawing on ancient insights from diverse cultures, they point to our much larger responsibility. We must halt human population growth not just to insure the well-being of humanity but to restore the interdependent biotic community in which we human beings must learn to see ourselves as members not masters.

THREE

A POWER-STRUCTURES
PERSPECTIVE

To understand why populations are exploding in the third world, one must come to see how choices open to people about their reproduction — those most personal, intimate choices — are influenced by structures of decision-making power. These structures include the distant arena of international finance and trade and extend downward to the level of national governments, on through the village, and, ultimately, to relationships within families.

"Power structures" is not a mysterious concept. We use it simply to refer to the rules, institutions, and assumptions that both determine who is allowed to participate in decisions and in whose interests decisions are made. The decisions most relevant to the population question are those governing access to and use of life-sustaining resources — land, jobs, health care, and the education needed to make the most of them — and contraceptive resources. (See figure 2 for a schematic representation of some of the many arenas of human relationships in which decisions are made that directly and indirectly influence fertility.)

Decision-making structures fall along a continuum from democratic to antidemocratic. By democratic we mean decision-making structures in which those most affected by the decisions participate or — at the very least — structures that include consideration of the interests of those affected. Of course, in no polity or other social institution is power shared in completely equal measure. But in our view, democratic organization exists to the extent that power is dispersed and no one is left utterly powerless. Antidemocratic structures, by contrast, can therefore be described as *nonparticipatory* — because those most affected have no say — or *unequal* —

FIGURE 2: Arenas of Decision-Making Power Influencing Fertility

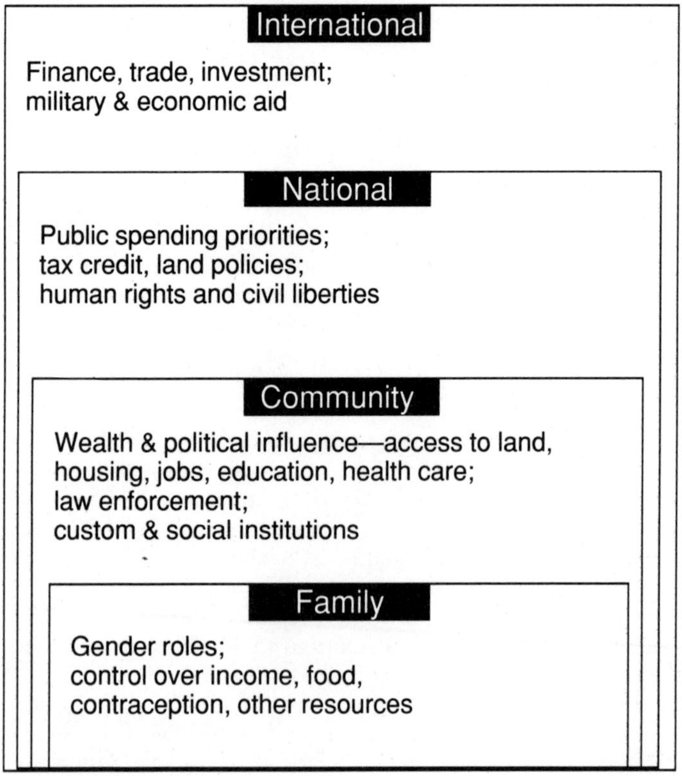

International

Finance, trade, investment;
military & economic aid

National

Public spending priorities;
tax credit, land policies;
human rights and civil liberties

Community

Wealth & political influence—access to land,
housing, jobs, education, health care;
law enforcement;
custom & social institutions

Family

Gender roles;
control over income, food,
contraception, other resources

when power is so concentrated that a few decide exclusively in
their own interests. *Our thesis is that antidemocratic power structures
create and perpetuate conditions keeping fertility high.*

In Western societies one tends to think of democracy as a political
concept; we think of power primarily as being exercised in the
political arena. Many Westerners also assume that in Marxist

theory, power is perceived differently — as largely an economic struggle over control of productive resources. And we in the West also assume that because the communist state is the antithesis of political democracy, any use of the term democratic is utterly inappropriate when describing communist societies.

But why restrict the use of the concepts of power and democracy? We find it most helpful to understand power as a critical variable in both political *and* economic affairs as well as in social and cultural life. And we find the terms *democratic* and *antidemocratic* — describing structures of decision-making power in a multiplicity of social institutions — most usefully applied not to societies in toto, but to the many arenas of life within societies.

It follows that we do not presume that within a society a uniform structure of power exists from the political to the economic to the social. While these varied aspects of community life interact and influence each other, asymmetry is more the norm. A society might be highly antidemocratic in the way political power is wielded but allow considerable sharing of economic control over essential resources. China comes to mind here. In contrast to most third world countries where the majority of rural people are denied control over basic resources, in China most rural people control enough land to secure their basic food needs. Even under the former collectivized system, everyone had the right to participate in economic life and share in the fruits from the land. At the same time, political leadership has not been freely chosen and people's right to political expression has not been protected.

The opposite imbalance is probably more common. In a number of societies — the United States is an example — political participation and expression are protected, but citizens' rights to economic resources essential for livelihood and healthcare are not protected. So a significant share of the population goes without enough income to provide adequate food, housing, and health care.

And while structures of economic and political power may be

relatively participatory at, say, the national political level, they may remain grossly unequal at another level — for example, when it comes to relations between men and women within the family.

In what follows we apply this power-structures perspective to the population problem. Power becomes the critical variable in explaining population growth patterns. Without it, it is possible to *describe* conditions like poverty associated with high fertility, but not to *understand* them or to arrive at workable solutions. In a report of this length, however, we can only sketch how structures of power — interpersonal to international — can influence reproductive choices.

In largely agrarian societies, the most clear-cut evidence of the economic power structure is who controls farmland and who does not. Access to land determines a family's survival and security. "Without land to feed my family, I go hungry, no matter how much food the country produces," one Indian peasant explained to us.

So, we must ask what are the consequences for fertility when at least 1 billion rural people in the third world have been deprived of farmland? In many countries, including Brazil, Mexico, the Philippines, India, and most of the Central American countries, landholdings have become increasingly concentrated in the hands of a minority during a period of rapid population growth. When the more powerful have an incentive to expand — say, to grow lucrative export crops — and have military backing, it is quite easy for them to seize the land of the less powerful. They might do it legally by calling in the loan of a heavily indebted peasant family, or, not so legally, by simply bulldozing the peasant's land and laying claim to it. The peasant family has no legal title nor lawyer to back up its claim in court.

In this context, without adequate land or secure tenure, and with no old-age support from the government or any other source outside the family, many poor people understandably view children as perhaps the only source of power open to them. For those in extreme poverty, children can be critical to one's very survival.

Children: Poor People's Source of Power

Living at the economic margin, many poor parents perceive their children's labor as necessary to augment meager family income. By working in the fields and around the home, children also free up adults and elder siblings to earn outside income.

One study on the island of Java, Indonesia, for example, found children to be an extremely important asset in the rural economy. As early as age seven, a boy assumes responsibility for his family's chicken and ducks. At nine, he can care for goats and cattle, cut fodder, and harvest and transplant rice. And as early as twelve, he can work for wages. And by his fifteenth birthday, a Javanese boy has, through his labor, repaid the entire investment his family has made in him.[15] Similarly in Bangladesh, by age six a son provides labor and/or income for his family. By twelve, at the latest, he contributes more than he consumes.[16]

The labor of girls is equally important. In Tanzania, one study found that girls between the ages of five and nine spend an average of three and a half hours a day working on economic activities and in the home.[17] In Peru, as in many other third world countries, girls of six and seven can be seen carting younger brothers and sisters around while their mothers are selling wares in the marketplace. And on tea plantations in India, girls as young as twelve rise at 4 a.m. to help their mothers prepare breakfast and then spend up to ten hours a day in the fields picking tea during harvest time.[18]

John Caldwell, a foremost theorist in population studies, criticizes his colleagues for underrating the importance of children to the village economy:

The analysis of the value of children in the village household economy often completely fails to understand the subsistence nature of village services.... [In Western] societies, most...expenditure is on goods...which merely occupy space while providing services. Vacuum cleaners pick up the dust; mowers keep down the grass; washing machines clean up the dishes; hot water systems provide hot water.... In a society where nearly all these consumer durables are vastly expensive and difficult or impossible to maintain, the services are largely provided by either cheap labour or more frequently by family subsistence labour.... *In terms of the availability of cheap or ostensibly free labour, the farmer would be irrational who forced himself and his family to produce ever more crops for sale to buy expensive gadgets to supply the services he could get directly [from his children].* [19]

And children aren't assets only for people living in the countryside, Caldwell points out. Among the Yoruba in Nigeria, urban white collar families rely on many children to enhance their position through "sibling assistance chains." As one child grows up and completes school, he or she (most often he!) can help younger siblings climb up the educational ladder. Each successive child is thus in a position to get a higher-paying job. The family gets added income, status, and security. [20]

Moreover, the "lottery mentality" is associated with poverty everywhere. With no reliable channels for advancement in sight, third world parents can always hope that the next child will be the one clever and bright enough to get an education and land a city job, despite the odds. In many countries, income from just one such job in the city can support a whole family in the countryside.

In nearly all third world societies, those rendered powerless by unjust economic structures also know that without children to care for them in old age, they will have nothing. [21] According to a 1984 World Bank report, 80 to 90 percent of the people surveyed in Indonesia, South Korea, Thailand, and Turkey expect to rely on their children for support in their old age. [22]

Page 22

In addition to providing old age security, children represent insurance against risk for many rural families, argues Mead Cain, a researcher at the Center for Population Studies in New York. Drawing on extensive experience in South Asia, Cain notes that children's financial help provide "an important means of insuring against property loss" to families for whom a bad crop year or unexpected expense can spell catastrophe, forcing a distress sale of their land. Only when other forms of economic security become available to impoverished families, posits Cain, will the transition to smaller families be instigated.[23]

Of course, the value of children to their parents cannot be measured just in hours of labor or extra income. The intangibles may be just as important. Influence within the community is one. In community affairs, bigger families can carry more weight. And for most parents, children offer incomparable satisfaction, fulfillment, and joy. For the poor—whose lives are marred by much more grief and sacrifice than is true of the better-off—the role children play in fulfilling these very real human needs cannot be underestimated.

The question of children's economic contributions to the family is not a settled one among population researchers, however. Recently some have begun to argue that the economic advantages children offer may be diminishing in ways that will reduce fertility. As primary and secondary education becomes more widespread, for instance, children have less time to contribute to their families.[24] Also, as more people lose or are unable to acquire land and migrate to the cities, they will take wage-paying jobs. For wage laborers, children come to represent a cost rather than just a benefit.

The Population Reference Bureau's Thomas Merrick uses this argument to help explain recent fertility declines in Mexico, Colombia, and Brazil. In each case, he argues, the economic squeeze reflected in declining real wages has made consumer aspirations more difficult to attain. In order to maintain their standard of living, however low, families react by limiting births.[25]

While the shift to wage labor and the simultaneous growth in third world cities may change the economic value of children for *some* families, we wonder whether it will have as dramatic an effect on fertility as Merrick and others assume. Before children can become a net drain on their wage-earning parents, those parents must have jobs. Yet in third world countries, vast numbers of urban people have not been able to find paid employment. So people find other ways to survive, and in many of these desperate strategies children are still assets. Children can engage in petty commerce, selling trinkets or snacks on the street. In the shantytowns of metropolitan Manila, whole families survive by collecting and selling scrap material from dumps. Children begging from tourists is another source of family income. And in the absence of alternatives, children also become prostitutes to support themselves and often their parents as well. Bangkok and Sao Paolo are both notorious for child prostitutes, many of whom are the sole supporters of their families.

When people are made powerless to provide for their children, children will continue to provide a primary way for parents, themselves, to survive.

When Many Babies Die

But to achieve any of the potential benefits of children, the third world poor realize that they need to have many. Where food resources and health care are the monopoly of the better-off, as many as one in every four children dies before the age of five (see table 2). Seeing their babies dying or their children in such poor health that the threat of death is ever present, parents naturally are motivated to have more children. In India, of the six or seven births women average, only four can be expected to survive.[26] One Sudanese doctor angrily described the problem:

In a country like ours where the infant mortality rate is 140 per 1,000 births, where infectious diseases kill so many children, where malnutrition affects about 30–50 percent of the people, where measles is a killer disease although it could be stopped by immunization, how can you tell us to stop having children? When a mother has twelve children, only three or four may live.[27]

Studies by the World Heath Organization confirm that both the actual death and the fear of death of a child will increase the fertility of a couple, regardless of income or family size.[28]

The positive impact of infant death on fertility rates is also a biological fact. Breastfeeding tends to prolong the period during which a woman cannot become pregnant, so that when her infant dies this infertile period is cut short. And this is no insignificant phenomenon. Lactation has been a primary means of birth spacing in many cultures, especially in Africa where babies have typically been breastfed for two years or longer.

Women: Powerlessness and High Birth Rates

High birth rates reflect not only the labor-income-security needs of the poor, but the disproportionate powerlessness of women. Excluded from many decisions that determine their role in the family, as well as in the society at large, many women have little opportunity for pursuits outside the home. Perpetual motherhood becomes their only "choice."

Perhaps the best proof that the powerlessness of women undergirds high fertility comes from extensive research on the effect of women's education. In one study after another, women's education turns out to be the single most consistent predictor of lower fertility. As women's schooling increases, fertility typically falls.

TABLE 2: Percentage of Children Who Do Not Survive to the Age of Five in Selected Countries

Country	%	Country	%
Afghanistan	33	Chad	23
Mali	30	Guinea-Bissau	23
Sierra Leone	30	Senegal	23
Malawi	27	Mauritania	22
Guinea	26	Kampuchea	22
Ethiopia	26	Liberia	21
Somalia	26	Rwanda	21
Mozambique	25	Yemen	21
Burkina Faso	24	Yemen, PDR	21
Angola	24	Bhutan	21
Niger	24	Nepal	21
Central African Republic	23	Burundi	20
		Bangladesh	20

SOURCE: UNICEF, *State of the World's Children*, 1987

Of course, few would interpret these findings literally — that women learn how to limit births. Rather, demographers surmise that the fact that women are getting educated reflects a multitude of changes in society that allow women greater power.

All this cuts to the core of the population issue because women's subordination to men within the family often translates into a direct loss of control over their own fertility. It has been widely documented that after several births many third world women want to avoid or delay pregnancy. But women simply do not have the power to act on their desire. As one doctor in a Mexican clinic explained:

When a wife wants to... [try] to limit the number of mouths to feed in the family, the husband will become angry and even beat her. He thinks it is unacceptable that she is making a decision of her own. She is challenging his authority, his power over her — and thus the very nature of his virility.[29]

Women who do try to limit their pregnancies — either with or without the consent of their partners — often receive little or no help from the state. Poor women have particularly limited access to health services, including birth control devices. In desperation, many resort to illegal, and often fatal, abortions. A major cause of maternal death in the third world,[30] complications from illegal abortions are estimated to kill over 200,000 women a year, most of them poor and illiterate third world women.[31]

Where a woman's choices are severely limited — where, for example, women are discouraged from working outside the home — children often represent her only source of power. In Kenya, population researchers note that the low status of women pushes them into early marriage and frequent childbearing.[32] "If society impedes other avenues to power such as pursuit of economic activity," point out two African scholars, "then women may compensate by having large numbers of children."[33] Sally Mugabe, writing in *Popline*, underscores the point:

> For a [Zimbabwean] woman, bearing and rearing children is the primary source of status in the family and the community. The larger number of children a woman has, the higher the status she enjoys.[34]

Other cultural forces severely limit a woman's freedom to choose fewer births. The influence of the Catholic church is significant in many countries. This is particularly true in Latin America. In the Institute for Food and Development Policy book *Don't Be Afraid, Gringo* a Honduran peasant woman talks in intimate detail about the many forces depriving her of the power to provide for her family. She reflects on why Honduran women have so many children:

> Not many campesina women use birth control. They just

keep having babies, babies, and more babies....I've thought a lot about why we have so many children....Part of the reason might be the Catholic church. Most of us are Catholics, and the church tells us that it's natural to have children and that going against nature is going against God.[35]

One can well imagine how difficult it is for Catholic women to use birth control if it means having to confess to a central authority figure in your community, the priest, that you have sinned. For many poor women, whose self-esteem is already low, challenging church authority can be virtually unthinkable.

The Fertility Consequences of Son Preference

Patriarchal family and community attitudes also pressure a woman to keep having children until she gives birth to a son, regardless of her own wishes or even possible jeopardy to her health. Male attitudes and power over women are critical. As we just noted, many women do not resist family planning, but as an Egyptian woman explains, it's the men "who are sometimes against it.... They want children until they get a boy."[36] In India, a preference for sons on the part of both parents is so strong that amniocentisis is now being used in many areas to determine the sex of the fetus. According to population researcher Betsy Hartmann, Indian women found to be carrying females are often pressured to abort by husbands and in-laws.[37] A study in Bombay of 8,000 abortions following amniocentisis found that all but *one* of the aborted fetuses were female.[38]

Son preference is not only linked to enhanced social status; it often has financial implications as well. China is a good example. A daughter offers her parents much less security than a son. Upon marriage, she leaves to live in her husband's home, whereas a son's wife comes to live with his parents, providing security and companionship in their old age. In Bangladesh, where many women are subject to the Islamic custom of Purdah (forbidden to leave, much less work, outside the home), the incentive is strong to bear sons for future social and economic support.[39] Sons can also better protect rights to the land, especially important to widows.[40]

Not Only Women Are Made Powerless

While the power-structures perspective helps explain the high birth rates of women subordinated within the family and society, it recognizes that often the men who hold power over women are themselves part of a subordinate group—those with little or no claim to income-producing resources. This, too, has important implications for fertility.

As long as poor men are denied sources of self-esteem through productive work, and are denied access to the resources they need to act responsibly toward their families, it's likely they will cling even more tenaciously to their superior power vis-à-vis women. For many men, this may mean showing their virility through siring large numbers of children. Men who are forced to migrate for work, for example, may decide to start up a second family, further increasing the number of children.

In many cultures, men unable to bring in enough income to support dependents feel inadequate to maintain a permanent household. The sad irony is that self-blame for this failure, lowering self-esteem, can result in a behavior pattern of moving in and out of relationships and the fathering of even more children.

Summarizing the Power-Structures Perspective

In our view, this varied evidence—drawn by anthropologists and sociologists working in the third world—about why the poor have many children, suggests that high fertility can best be understood as a response to antidemocratic structures of power within which people are often left with little choice but many births.

To recap, freedom of choice in fertility is nonexistent where:

- one's financial security depends entirely or largely on one's surviving children
- many births are necessary to ensure that even several children live to maturity
- health services, including birth control, are available almost exclusively to the better-off in urban areas, not to the poor
- a woman has no choice other than marriage and her only source of power is derived from her children, especially sons
- few opportunities for education and employment exist for women outside of homemaking

Thus the power-structures analysis — particularly in recent years[41] — stresses the impact on fertility of women's subordination to men, a condition that contributes to the social pressure for many births. But it places this problem within the context of unjust economic structures that deny people realistic alternatives to unlimited reproduction. Within such a framework, rapid population growth is seen to result largely from efforts by the poor to cope, given their powerlessness in the face of the concentrated economic strength of an elite.

Thus, the narrowly constricted power of third world women can only be understood in light of relationships extending far beyond the family and even the community (again, see figure 2). From the level of international trade and finance, down to jobs and income available to men as well as women, antidemocratic structures of decision making set limits on people's choices which ultimately influence their reproductive options.

In a report of this length, we can only offer a few examples to suggest how decisions at these many levels can affect fertility.

At the international level, consider the debt crisis. In the 1970s, third world governments received large loans from banks in the industrial nations, investing the money in big-ticket projects — airports, arms, nuclear power plants, and so on — responding to the interests of their wealthiest citizens. In the 1980s, many of these loans came due, just as interest rates climbed and prices of raw material exports from the third world hit a thirty-year low. As a result, between 1982 and 1987, the net transfer from poor countries to banks and governments in the rich countries totalled $140 billion, or the equivalent of *two* Marshall Plans. [42]

How did third world countries come up with such sums? Health and welfare budgets and food subsidies got slashed first. And to earn foreign exchange land and credit increasingly went toward export crops. But reduced health care budgets means that more babies die and fewer resources are available for comprehensive family planning care. More resources devoted to crops for export means that locally, food becomes more scarce and more expensive. Add to this cuts in government food subsidies. Understandably, nutrition and health worsen; death rates rise. The link between debt and heightened death rates is so clear that sociologists have quantified it: every additional $10 in interest paid per person per year by seventy-three poor countries means 142 days shorter life on average than would be true if life expectancy had continued to improve at pre-debt levels. [43]

Thus, the "international debt crisis" — seemingly remote from intimate reproductive behavior — ends up affecting conditions of basic family security, health, and nutrition known to influence fertility. High growth rates can in part be understood by reference to such far-reaching decisions that end up shifting resources away from the poor. From this analysis, one can surmise that in a country like the debt-burdened Philippines, the disappointing stall in the decline in birth rates is in part due to the increasing insecurity of the poor whose lives have become even less secure in the last decade.

Government policies directly affect the poor majority's access to land, and thus influence the peasant family's sense of security which plays a part in its child-bearing choices (see figure 2). In many countries, including the Philippines, El Salvador, and Brazil, for example, agrarian policy is beholden to the most wealthy landowners. They have made sure to block reforms transferring land to the poorest peasants. In Brazil, for example, 224 large farms still control as much land as 1.7 million peasant families.[44] Given what we now know about how the insecurity of landlessness affects poor families' view of their need for children, it should come as no surprise that in such countries fertility remains high.

Honduras offers another illustration. After Haiti, it is the poorest country in the western hemisphere. In 1980, two-thirds of its national budget was devoted to economic and social programs and one-third to debt repayment and defense. But in the 1980s, Honduras became a central staging ground for U.S. military operations in Central America. Millions in U.S. military aid went to Honduras and the government was pressured to increase its own military expenditures. By 1984, Honduras' budget priorities were completely reversed: education, housing, health and other such programs received only a third of the budget. The rest went to debt and the military. Given the link between improved health and education and fertility, it is clear that the geopolitical strategy of a foreign power–diverting the Honduran government from social programs — is powerfully influencing its potential to reduce its high birth rate.[45]

We've only sketched some of the layers of decision making power shaping human reproductive life, but the reader might draw back with skepticism. Does not such a far-reaching approach confuse more than clarify — for could not virtually every economic, political, and cultural fact of life be squeezed into such a broad perspective?

Our response is that to achieve a holistic understanding one's view must necessarily be far reaching. But this does not mean that it is without coherency. The pivot on which our perspective turns is the concept of power, a concept that we have found woefully missing in the perspectives we earlier critiqued. Without such a concept, we believe it is impossible to understand the complex and interacting problems of poverty, hunger, and population, much less act effectively to address them.

FOUR

THE DEBATE ABOUT SOLUTIONS

As we opened this report, we outlined four perspectives on the population problem. Because the problem is defined in such profoundly different ways, it should come as no surprise that proposed solutions vary as drastically.

Do nothing — the market will provide. The first "solution" is simply not to perceive rapid population growth as a problem — the Julian Simon approach. According to Simon, we need no solution as long, that is, as we allow the market mechanism to operate freely. The market will spur human creativity to discover or create ever-new resources for human betterment. We reject this perspective because of its narrow focus on the human species.

Let nature take its course. Biological determinists such as Garrett Hardin argue that if third world governments are unwilling to take the action necessary to bring birth rates down, we must let nature take its course. Where rampant hunger and environmental devastation prove that populations have overrun their carrying capacities, the only humane solution is to let them starve. Intervening to try to save lives now will only lead to greater suffering later as even more people press against a depleted resource base.

Sending food aid is the most misguided form of altruism because it perpetuates people's suffering, according to Hardin. Populations must be allowed to die back to levels sustainable by local resources. Immigration from "overpopulated" countries must not be allowed either, lest it interfere with this natural balancing of population and its habitat.

Largely because of the moral repugnance this view evokes, it has few adherents. But the fallacies in its logic must be challenged. Widespread hunger is no measure of overpopulation — as the biological determinist assumes — when in a Brazil or a Zaire, plentiful resources per capita exist beside severe hunger. Even Ethiopia, Hardin's favorite example of overpopulation, could feed itself if resources were equitably and wisely developed. Geographers and other social scientists also point out that linking the biological concept of carrying capacity to the boundaries of the nation-state is not particularly meaningful in the first place. What is natural about people being forced to support themselves within the limits of a humanmade and an ecologically arbitrary political unit, they ask.

Certainly many industrial countries hardly live from their own resource bases. Japan is a particularly dramatic example of a society heavily dependent on imported foodstuffs, but few biological determinists appear ready to declare that the Japanese must die back to the carrying capacity of their islands.

Family planning is the only hope. In searching for solutions, the two perspectives we earlier called the "food-versus-resources perspective" and the "social perspective" merge. Both now acknowledge that poor people have many children as part of a survival strategy and that women often give birth to many children because they lack alternative sources of status and security. Yet most mainstream population organizations appear unwilling to address the roots of these problems that lie largely in the economic and political order. When it comes to action toward solutions, the focus narrows to family planning. A leading demographer can write, for example, that "98 percent of the resources and effort should be devoted to social and economic development"[46] but it's on the remaining two percent — population control — that he and his organization choose to focus their work.

Why are the social causes downplayed or forgone when it comes to a program of action?

For many, no doubt, an unwillingness to devote resources to attacking the underlying social causes of rapid population growth flows from feelings of impotency in face of the deeper causal forces, coupled with a sense of urgency. They have, in effect, responded: "We can't bring about societywide changes benefiting the poor and we can't wait for others to achieve this goal for themselves. All this would take too long anyway. The population bomb is exploding *now.*"

Once in this frame of mind, appropriate action seems obvious. All we in the industrial countries can do is fund ever-more-stringent population control programs in the third world. In 1984, Walter Holzhausen, Bangladesh representative for the UN Development Program wrote:

> No one really doubts the need for massive direct or indirect intervention by government to limit the size of families; nor does anyone seriously believe that Bangladesh has the money or the time to establish better [mother-child health care] services and better educational facilities as a precondition for making voluntary family planning more successful.[47]

Also couching her views in hard-nosed realism, the Worldwatch Institute's Jodi Jacobson concludes in a 1987 report that economically depressed third world governments "can no longer rely on socioeconomic gains to help reduce births."[48] Jacobson acknowledges the "social conditions underlying high fertility... includ[ing] the low status of women, and the illiteracy, low wages, and ill health that customarily accompany it." But, unwilling to face the logical implication that it is *this* reality that must be addressed, she resorts to a non sequitur and simply exhorts governments confronted by fast-growing populations "to promote family planning to establish a balance between numbers of people and available resources."[49]

Many defending family planning as virtually the only feasible line of attack on high birth rates also imply directly or by their silence that those living outside a fast-growing country cannot address the deeper, social roots of its population problem. Outsiders cannot reform the economic and political structures of other societies, it is assumed. This position ignores the many channels — diplomatic, military, commercial, financial (detailed in our discussion of figure 2) — through which outsiders *already* greatly influence the structures of decision making power affecting fertility within many third world countries.

Having rejected the possibility of addressing the underlying social roots of high birth rates — it takes too long, poor countries can't afford it, and we can't tell them what to do anyway — what is left? Family planning. All one can do is to fund family planning services and education, sponsor research on more effective contraceptives, and gently advise foreign governments about the need for family planning programs. To do this, national and international population agencies argue they need more money, more personnel, and a greater political commitment to family planning activities. In the last twenty years, the governments and organizations in the industrialized countries have spent $4 billion on third world population control.[50]

The Consequences of Focusing Narrowly on Family Planning

The promotion of family planning programs in the third world sounds beneficent. Indeed, we have stressed all along that access to birth control is essential both to the empowerment of women and reducing birth rates. But we observe a critical difference between those family planning programs developed as part of an overall attack on the social forces keeping birth rates high and, by contrast, programs that promote family planning as an *alternative to social change*.

It is this later approach that we find both ethically questionable and self-defeating. Once the social roots of high fertility are deemed impossible to address and fewer births becomes *the* goal, noble ends get sacrificed to dubious means. Many women are hurt in the process, and ultimately even the end itself — halting population growth — is unattainable.

This is a controversial statement with far-reaching implications. So let us explain what brings us to this conclusion.

The argument that it is not possible to address the social conditions leading to high birth rates, but that it is possible to reduce growth rates anyway, starts with evidence of unmet demand for contraception. Those focusing on family planning cite data showing that in many third world countries almost half of all women of child-bearing age want no more children but lack access to birth control. Fertility rates would drop by a third if we could just meet this unmet need, they claim. [51]

This argument entails a big assumption: without altering social conditions — especially the powerlessness of women vis-à-vis men and the meager access of the poor to security resources — women will in fact be able to *act* on their stated desire for fewer children. But might many women indeed declare their preference for fewer children yet lack the power to act on their preference — *even if* the technical means of birth control were available? In other words, to believe that the mere provision of contraception will suddenly allow women to step out of their subordinate role in the family, or alter the fact that children still represent a source of security for many third world parents, is to ignore the findings of decades of fertility-oriented research.

Moreover, if unmet demand were truly as great as it is assumed, why, we ask, have population planners had to resort to incentives and disincentives? In some cases, downright coercion has been deemed necessary to get people to accept birth control, suggesting that people must be made to override their own judgments about their need for children.

Manipulating Contraceptive Demand

As part of their single-minded effort to promote birth control in the third world, many international agencies, together with willing third world governments, have not only sought to respond to existing contraceptive demand, but have actively worked to increase it. While some strategies are relatively innocuous — television soap operas promoting new family size norms — in at least a dozen countries, mainly in Asia, a variety of incentives and disincentives are now used to induce people to undergo sterilization or to use contraception.[52] Incentives are usually material. They range from payments to the individual, family, or family planning clinic to awards of small farm animals, clothes, and even food. Disincentives also tend to be financial: tax differentials (higher taxes after a certain number of children), employment policies (restrictions on maternity leave), or limitations on social services, such as health or education.

India. During the 1976–1977 "emergency" in which constitutional rights were suspended, the Indian government embarked on a major campaign to lower its birth rate, mainly relying on sterilization.[53] In some Indian states, civil servants were financially penalized for not meeting specified targets, and parents with three or more children who didn't undergo sterilization were denied loans, food rations, land for housing, and free medical treatment at government hospitals.[54] There were even reports of men being rounded up off the street in some villages and given vasectomies by overzealous government employees trying to meet their quotas.[55]

Under heavy attack for these harsh actions, the Indian government tried to reduce abuses by instituting financial incentives; however, abuses appear still to be common.[56] Individuals agreeing to undergo sterilization are currently compensated by an amount equal to ten to twelve days' wages; compensation for a sterilization is fifteen times as high as it is for accepting an IUD. The central government also gives each state money for every person who gets sterilized (30 rupees per woman and 40 rupees per man).[57] "Especially in tribal areas where there is widespread poverty and starvation," notes one respected Indian population specialist, "the cash incentives provided can be considered coercive."[58]

Certain state governments in India have passed some of these incentives on to local promoters. In Maharashtra, for instance, district officials and leaders who achieve unusually high contraceptive acceptance rates are sent on a foreign tour.[59]

Bangladesh. Under the government's incentive program, both men and women are given a free piece of clothing, dubbed "surgical apparel," and are paid 175 taka for being sterilized, equal to two weeks' earnings.[60] As in many other countries, doctors and clinic staff also receive a payment for each sterilization they perform and until recently stood to lose wages and even their jobs for failing to meet monthly quotas. Moreover, to spread the inducements beyond the health care system, the government pays a special fee to anyone "referring" or "motivating" someone to undergo sterilization.[61]

All these programs are dubbed "voluntary" by their defenders. But when one is hungry, how many choices are voluntary? In Bangladesh, where the majority are desperately poor, sterilizations rose dramatically when incentives were increased in 1983. Most telling, sterilizations tend to fluctuate with the availability of food. In 1984, during the flood months of July to October, according to the *Bangladesh Observer*, sterilizations rose to an unprecedented quarter million, or almost one-fourth of all sterilizations performed during the entire decade 1972-1982.[62] In some cases, it was found that both a husband and wife had undergone sterilizations in order to receive the incentive payment![63]

The system of incentives invites abuse, argues author Betsy Hartmann, who has lived and worked in Bangladesh. In 1984, for instance, donations of wheat to the poor in the aftermath of severe flooding in several areas were made conditional on women agreeing to sterilization. After the operation, each woman received a certificate signed by a family planning officer vouching for her sterility and entitling her to a sari, money, and wheat.[64]

Thailand and Indonesia. Not all incentives are targeted at individuals. In poverty-ridden, northeastern Thailand, family planning is combined with government programs offering technical and financial support for animal raising, agricultural activities, environmental projects, and home industry.[65] And in Indonesia, the government has given public recognition and prizes — including public meeting halls, road repairs, and a clean water supply[66] — to communities meeting fertility targets or outdoing other locales in controlling births.[67]

But such programs raise a curious question. Why weren't government programs aimed at improving the lives of the poor adopted long ago as part of government's responsibility to its people? If it takes the threat of uncontrolled population growth to motivate attention to such concerns, we question how systemic and effective the poverty-alleviating programs will be. Such programs also raise the ethical question of whether citizens' access to such life necessities as clean water should hinge upon a community's reproductive record.

Upping the Contraceptive Ante

There are further serious implications in any strategy to slow population growth that does not at the same time ameliorate poor living conditions.

Birth control options shrink to those that don't require sanitary conditions or even clean water, cutting out the safest type of birth control of all, the barrier methods. Moreover, without changes underway in the community to make more open and equal the relations between men and women, population planners will lean toward techniques that do not require the cooperation, or even the approval, of men. Again, under these conditions, the safest methods — condoms and diaphragms — are given short shrift or dismissed as impractical.

Finally, without progress in providing comprehensive primary health care able to adapt contraceptives to individual women's needs and to deal with side effects, it is easy to rationalize the promotion of technologies that require no individualized application and cannot be readily rejected by women when problems do arise. Studies show high contraceptive rejection rates in the third world: 20 to 40 percent of women using the IUD or the pill discontinue use in the first year.[68] Long-term, injectable contraceptives, however, cannot be rejected between doses. Thus these long-acting contraceptives are fast gaining ground in third world population control programs. Among family planning officials, feelings of urgency about the population crisis and impotency about alternative approaches no doubt further justify the promotion of these more powerful interventions.

In sum, if the social realities women face are not changing, family planners will be motivated to push the most long-lasting contraceptives, removing from women the option of interrupting use. And, as we explain below, these are also the least safe methods. In other words, once one accepts the position that family planning is virtually all that we can — and must — do to bring population growth rates down, it follows that ever more coercive and intrusive strategies will be designed to reduce births.

In fact, those who strongly advocate family planning as a solution, inadvertently admit much of the argument we have just made. Once accepting as irremedial the social realities in which women are forced to live, the only alternative is long-acting birth control methods. Jacobson writes:

In many cultures... the diaphragm is considered undesirable because women are uncomfortable using this method. It may also be impractical where water for washing is in short supply.

Though the pill is relatively inexpensive, it may be a highly ineffective method where primary health care is poor and contraceptive supplies uncertain. And unexpected or unpleasant side effects can cause considerable anxiety among women in countries where medical advice is hard to come by.... Long acting, inexpensive birth control methods are more likely to serve the needs of low-income consumers in developing countries.[69]

Resigned to ever more potent birth control technologies as the only tool with which to bring birth rates down, many governments and international agencies have placed effectiveness ahead of women's safety. Arguing that poor health and sanitation conditions — as well as limited education — make it difficult for third world peoples to use barrier methods like the diaphragm, condoms, and spermicidal foams, family planning advocates have pushed for the use of longer-term, more "effective" methods like IUDs, injectable contraceptives, and sterilization.

One example of a contraceptive whose long-term effects are unknown is the injectable Depo-provera, one dose of which can prevent pregnancy for three to six months. Although judged too hazardous for general use in the United States,[70] family planning agencies promote Depo-provera in over eighty other countries.[71] An estimated 5 to 10 million women have already used the drug; in Thailand alone, a million injections have been given.[72] Known, short-term side effects include menstrual disorders, headaches, weight gain, depression, loss of libido, abdominal discomfort, and delayed return to fertility.[73] Preliminary studies suggest that Depo-provera may also be linked to an increased long-term risk of cervical cancer.[74]

Many, including some third world women, have been quick to point out that Depo-provera has important benefits to women — preventing unwanted and possibly dangerous pregnancies — which may well outweigh its risks. But the individual user can only make such a choice once she has all the facts. Yet seldom do doctors and family planning staff give third world women the full information they need to make an informed judgment. Depo-provera also reduces a woman's options in the sense that once the shot is given she cannot change her mind for the three to six months it takes for the effects to wear off.

In the Philippines, researcher Lynn Duggan asked the staff of one family planning clinic (funded by the International Planned Parenthood Federation) whether they routinely told their clients of the U.S. ban on the drug's use as a contraceptive. "Of course not," was the reply.[75] Nor is it unusual for women to remain uninformed about the drug's side effects, says Duggan.[76]

The South African government has commonly abused Depo-provera in its effort to control the size of the black population. According to a medical student from that country, black women are given the shot against their will, often without any explanation as to its nature or purpose.[77] Every three months, family planning teams funded by the South African government visit factories and farms just to administer the injection to women. Those who refuse may be subject to dismissal. Having a family planning card as proof of one's "protection" is mandatory for any black woman seeking a job in a factory or as a domestic worker.[78]

One of the newest long-acting contraceptives is Norplant, described as "the most effective contraceptive yet developed."[79] Implanted beneath a woman's skin, Norplant works like a time-release capsule preventing pregnancy for five or more years. Though Norplant has not yet been approved for use in the United States, it is legally available in ten countries, including Colombia, China, Finland, Sweden, Thailand, Indonesia, and Ecuador.[80] One likely advantage, at least from a family planning agency's perspective, is its price tag: Norplant costs as little as $2.80 per year of protection, a figure that is expected to fall as production increases.[81]

According to its promoters, Norplant's hormonal dose is smaller than the pill's or Depo-provera's; it has shown no adverse effect on future fertility and has a very low failure rate.[82] Yet the list of short-term side effects are not unlike those we noted for Depo-provera.[83] Moreover, because Norplant should only be implanted and removed by trained medical personnel under sterile conditions, a woman who changes her mind about getting pregnant is at the mercy of her country's health care system. For third world women, finding qualified medical help can be a tough challenge. In Jakarta, Indonesia, for example, a city of 12.8 million people, only one facility is equipped to remove Norplant.[84]

Family planners defend long-lasting contraceptives because they are said to be cost-effective and carefree, demanding little attention from the user. But precisely because of these factors, the new technology can actually reduce instead of enhance a woman's choice if reversal depends on scarce medical personnel or if the new technology delays the return of a woman's fertility, even after disuse.

Sterilization, because it is usually irreversible in women, is the final step in removing choice. And it is becoming increasingly popular among population agencies. In India, for instance, fully 90 percent of the couples practicing contraception have now been sterilized;[85] and Mexican sterilization rates have jumped over 300 percent in only six years.[86] (In fact, as of 1982, over half of all married Mexican women practicing birth control had been sterilized, given injectables, or fitted with an IUD.)[87]

Puerto Rico, however, may be the most extreme example of government programs restricting rather than expanding choice. Worried by rising unemployment as Puerto Rico moved toward a capital-intensive, export economy, the government began promoting sterilization as early as the mid-1940s.[88] A major propaganda campaign, using radio, television, and other forms of media sought to convince women to get "la operacion." In one poster put out by the Puerto Rican National Planning Institute, a mass of people are tangled together fighting to get out. "Let's Plan Today in Order to Avoid This Disaster in the Future" reads the caption.[89]

By 1965, Puerto Rico had the highest sterilization rate in the world: one-third of all ever-married women had been sterilized, two-fifths of them before the age of 25.[90]

The Puerto Rican government has never actively supported birth control clinics supplying other methods.[91] So today contraceptive choice remains limited to sterilization or the pill. Barrier methods such as the diaphragm, condoms, and foam are difficult to obtain.[92]

Women's organizations attack the Puerto Rican sterilization program as the most abusive in the world. Not only were many Puerto Rican women never told that the operation was essentially irreversible, but some were even unknowingly sterilized while under anesthesia for another operation.[93]

Health Risks and Third World Realities

These long-lasting methods also entail more health risks. Although sterilization is usually considered relatively safe for both men and women, given the lack of sterile conditions for surgery in many third world clinics, sterilization can be dangerous. Alarmed by an avoidable 1987 death of a woman from infection following sterilization, a women's health group in Bangladesh called on the government to put concern for women's health first. Shareen Hoq, a leader of the organization, told the press:

> We're really concerned with the lack of emphasis on safety in the government [family planning] program....Money spent on incentives is money that should be spent on improving health care for women who choose to be sterilized. Now, the government seems to think a form of birth control is "safe" if it's effective — in other words, that the woman definitely won't get pregnant. In that sense, sterilization in considered "safest." But we're talking about real safety — about not jeopardizing women's lives for the sake of reaching a quota.[94]

While health care is hard to come by for most third world women and completely out of reach for many, the side effects of contraceptives may affect third world women more severely than they typically affect women in the industrial countries. The overall health of third world women is likely to be much poorer, with lower resistance to infection and higher incidence of anemia, making loss of blood more serious. Thus safe use of contraceptives may require *even more* health care attention for third world women than would be needed by women in the industrial countries. Earlier we quoted Elvia Alvarado, a Honduran peasant. Again she describes her own experience:

> My daughters take birth control. I told my daughter Clara that her husband is too poor for her to have another child right now. But to tell you the truth, I don't like my daughters using birth control, because of all the problems it causes. Those pills do a lot of harm to women here. Maybe they don't affect the gringas [North American women] so much, because they are more resistant than we are. They are stronger and better fed. But not Honduran women; many of them get sick.

> Methods like the IUD give lots of infections. And you have to remember that when we get sick it's hard for us to get to a doctor. The nearest clinic is far away. And even if we could see a doctor, we can't afford to buy the medicine. I know a woman who had to pay $60 to get rid of an infection in her vagina. That's more than most of us make in a month![95]

A final point about safety: the availability of safe and legal abortion helps to make possible birth control alternatives with fewer health risks. That is, if abortion is available as a last resort if birth control fails, women are more likely to feel they can opt for the safer barrier methods of contraception which nonetheless entail a greater risk of pregnancy. Thus the U.S. government's position of denying support for family planning programs that offer abortion, directly undercuts women's ability to choose safer birth control methods.

The ethical issues raised here are extremely difficult to sort out. But before going on, let us summarize the questions we have touched on. While we advocate family planning, we believe that critical questions must be raised in evaluating population programs:

- Do they enhance the self-determination and well-being of women, or do they remove control of fertility from women, placing it in the hands of health care — or more accurately, birth control — providers?

- Do they offer ongoing, village-level care needed to assist people in choosing appropriate methods and in dealing safely with side effects?

- And answers to these questions in large part turn on another all important one: Does a government view population control as a means of reducing social pressures resulting from economic and political inequities that it is unwilling to confront? In other words, is population control a *substitute* for economic and political reform responsive to the needs of the poor?

How Far Can Birth Control Alone Take Us?

Even if population control advocates are willing to ignore the wealth of evidence showing why fertility rates remain high and plunge ahead with ever more intrusive and coercive methods of family planning, we ask, what will this buy the third world country or the world community? Are birth rates likely to fall to replacement levels, and if so, what is the price — the ethical and human costs — we must pay?

First, how much are birth rates likely to drop in the absence of other changes leading to more democratic power structures?

A number of demographers have sought to isolate the impact of family planning programs on fertility, independent of what we would consider key indicators of poor peoples' relative power, i.e., literacy and educational levels, life expectancy, and infant mortality rates. But virtually all have run into a similar snag: family planning programs and these social realities are almost nowhere independent. Sociologist Phillips Cutright explains:

> The very question of whether a family planning program can produce fertility declines in the absence of development is a straw man, since... socioeconomic development — in the form of health and educational development — is a prerequisite for the creation of a strong family planning program.[96]

In fact, the main conclusion of most of these studies is that while family planning programs do have some effect on fertility over and above improvements in social and economic conditions, the two work best together. "Countries that rank well on socioeconomic variables and also make substantial [family planning] program effort," write the authors of a widely respected study on this issue, "have on average much more fertility decline than do countries that have one or the other, and far more than those with neither."[97] They also note that for countries at the bottom of the socioeconomic scale, the probable impact on contraceptive use of simply adopting a family planning program would be slight.[98]

The experience of the Indian state of Kerala confirms the importance of socioeconomic change in reducing fertility. Kerala has had a family planning program since the mid-1960s, which certainly aided in its fertility decline. But not until social conditions were ripe did people turn to modern contraception.[99] "In Kerala," notes K. C. Zachariah, population analyst at the World Bank, "the steps came in the right order — a reduction in infant and child mortality, accompanied or followed by an increase in female education, followed by redistributive policies and finally by the official family planning program."[100]

Kerala's success with family planning is especially striking when compared to the rest of India. As we noted earlier, the Indian government launched its most comprehensive nationwide family planning campaign in the mid-1970s. Interestingly, however, the fall in Indian fertility doesn't appear to have been hastened by the program; in fact the decline in India's total fertility rates between 1975 and 1985 was virtually the same as it was a decade earlier — about 15 percent over each ten year period.[101] And, according to the latest figures, the downward trend in Indian fertility seems to have slowed considerably.[102]

While a number of poor countries have achieved major reductions in fertility without significantly improving the security of the majority of citizens — Thailand, Indonesia, and Mexico being three examples — none has come close to halting population growth. Nor is there much likelihood, given current trends, that they can do so in the near future. In fact, among low-income countries, aside from some small island populations, only China and Cuba have reached or nearly reached an annual increase as low as 1 percent. China has had a government-sponsored family program for some time; Cuba has not. The Cuban government provides contraceptives, including abortion, through its free health care system, but has never undertaken an organized family planning campaign. However, both countries have addressed the structural roots of insecurity and opened opportunities to women outside the home.

Highlighting the fact that family planning programs *in and of themselves* have not had a dramatic impact on reducing fertility does not mean that we belittle their value. Making contraceptives widely available and helping to reduce inhibitions against their use are critical to the goal of greater human freedom — especially the freedom of women — as well as essential to halting population growth.

Can Reducing Population Growth Alleviate Hunger and Other Social Problems?

The power structures analysis poses one additional question to those advocating family planning as a means of enhancing human well-being and alleviating stress on the environment: Can reducing births reduce poverty, hunger, and environmental degradation? Since rapid population growth is not the cause of these closely intertwined problems, we doubt that simply slowing growth can alleviate them.

Consider a few of the countries that have managed to reduce birth rates without significantly redistributing access to survival resources — land, jobs, and health care.

In Mexico, for example, despite a 37 percent decline in fertility rates since 1960, there is little evidence that the people are any less hungry.[103] Data on malnutrition indicate that fully a fifth of all Mexicans are malnourished, with the estimates ranging as high as 40 to 60 percent for children under four in Mexico's rural areas.[104]

The estimates refer to the late 1970s — well *after* Mexico's fertility decline was underway[105] and at a time when the country was still experiencing an economic boom from oil exports. The economic crisis of the 1980s has made life harder for many Mexicans and falling fertility has provided no measurable relief for Mexico's poor.[106]

Thailand's experience is similar. In part because of an effective family planning program, Thailand's fertility rates have been cut in half since 1960. But according to a 1984 survey conducted by the Thai Ministry of Health, over half of all children under five suffer from malnutrition — equivalent to 3.3 million children.[107] Malnutrition has been increasing despite both lowered birth rates and improved agricultural production.[108] Thailand is not only a major net exporter of rice, the country's main staple food, but of meat, corn, cassava, beans, sugar cane, and many fruits and vegetables, all of which could be used for domestic consumption.[109] Most of Thailand's hunger results from highly skewed farmland ownership, especially in the central plain, where land is most productive.[110]

India is yet another example. India's fertility rates—while still comparatively high—have declined 32 percent in twenty-five years.[111] Yet is the Indian population any better fed? Despite the country's dramatic economic and industrial development of the last several decades, the majority of the population has not benefited economically. Nearly half the population lacks the income necessary to buy a nutritious diet.[112] Its own people's widespread hunger notwithstanding, India actually exports food; in 1984, its net agricultural exports were worth almost $1 billion.[113]

It could be argued, of course, that without a slowdown in population growth in such countries, the poor majorities would be still worse off. Even more people would be going hungry, and more families would be without jobs or land.

Stepping back for a minute to consider the deeper implications of this argument—that all we can do is to reduce the rate of population growth today so things won't be worse for even more people tomorrow—we see that it leads to an untenable moral stance. Can we ethically claim success if we hold the number of hungry people in the world to 700 million? Obviously not. The moral imperative is clear. We cannot let ourselves get sidetracked from addressing the undemocratic power structures that give rise to the problems of poverty, environmental destruction, and population growth by "solutions" which at best can only limit the numbers hurt.

An analogy may be useful. Imagine that you have a disease, which is slowly getting worse. You approach your doctor for help. After examining you, the doctor offers some not-very-comforting news. "I can offer a treatment that will stop the spread of the disease, but I can't prescribe the cure." He openly admits that the cure is well-known, but unfortunately for you, it is only approved for use in certain countries and yours is not among them. Besides, he is not licensed to give it to you anyway — it's not in his specialty.

Given the seriousness of the population problem for our whole planet, we cannot rationalize dispensing a less effective medicine in the presence of a known cure. Yet such a course is in effect what is being promoted by those who claim that in certain countries there is no hope for social and economic change.

Solutions from the Power-Structures Perspective

An alternative approach to solutions flows from what we have called the power-structures perspective on the population problem.

In this perspective, rapid population growth is a *moral* crisis because it reflects the widespread denial of essential human rights to survival resources — land, food, jobs — and the means to prevent pregnancy. A power-structures perspective therefore holds that far- reaching economic and political change is necessary to reduce birth rates to replacement levels. Such change must enhance the power of the poorest members of society, removing their need to cope with economic insecurity by giving birth to many children. Social arrangements beyond the family — jobs, health care, old-age security, and education (especially for women) — must offer both security and opportunity.

In this process, education is key to opportunity. As the opportunity for primary and secondary education becomes more widespread, taking children away from family support activities, the immediate economic value of children to the family will diminish.

Second, the power of women must be augmented through expanded opportunities for both men and women.

Third, limiting births must become a viable option by making *safe and acceptable* birth control devices universally available.

Family planning cannot by itself reduce population growth, though it can speed a decline; it best contributes to a demographic transition when integrated into village-and neighborhood-based health systems that offer birth control to expand human freedom rather than to control behavior.

To test this thesis as to the cause of rapid population growth and its implied prescriptions, we have looked critically at population trends over the last twenty years. The historical evidence appears to bear it out. Consider the implications of the following statistics covering three-fourths of the world's people who live in some seventy-odd countries the World Bank designates low and lower-middle income.[114]

Lessons from Seven Successful Societies

While average annual population growth rates in all industrial countries have been below 2 percent a year for decades, among the more than seventy poor countries only six had both reduced their population growth to less than 2 percent by the period 1980-1985 and cut total fertility rates by a third or more since 1960. They are China, Sri Lanka, Colombia, Chile, Burma, and Cuba (see table 3).[115] Although not a country, and therefore not listed in the World Bank statistics, the Indian state of Kerala also meets these criteria.[116]

Population growth in these six countries plus India's Kerala state has slowed at a much faster rate than in the current industrialized countries during their transition from high to low growth.[117] What do these exceptions tell us? What could societies as different as

TABLE 3: Population Success Stories

Country	Population Growth Rate 1980–1985 %	Total Fertility Decline 1960–1985 %
Burma	2.0	35.0
Colombia	1.9	50.7
Kerala (India)	1.8[a]	38.0[b]
Chile	1.7	51.0
Sri Lanka	1.4	38.5
China	1.2	35.3
Cuba	0.8	53.5

SOURCES: World Bank, *World Development Report*, 1987, 254–255. Data for Kerala from K. C. Zachariah "The Anamoly of the Fertility Decline in Kerala's India State," *World Bank Staff Working Paper* no. 700, Population and Development Series no. 75, 1984, 45. Data represent statistics from three districts in Kerala.

a Average for years 1971–1981.
b 1965/1970–1975/1980

those of China, Sri Lanka, Chile, Colombia, Cuba, Burma, and Kerala have in common?

Is it that they have carried out the most aggressive family planning programs? In general, no. Some have and some have not.

A 1985 study rated most third world countries according to what demographers call "family planning effort," the prevalence and strength of organized family planning programs. The study included six of the countries we are focusing on here; Kerala was not included because it is not a country. It found that Chile and Burma had weak or very weak family planning efforts; Cuba showed moderate effort; and China, Sri Lanka, and Colombia showed strong effort.[118]

Our thesis suggests, moreover, that even those three societies in which family planning effort has been strong could not have succeeded nearly as well as they have without social changes allowing people to take advantage of their birth control programs. Thus the striking parallels among these disparate societies lie in just such social changes.

First, four of the seven have assured their citizens considerable security through access to a basic diet. They have had more extensive food guarantee systems than exist in other third world societies.

China. Since the early 1950s, every rural family has had access to land and its fruits, and city dwellers were assured a minimum food allotment. At least until very recently, families unable to earn enough through their own labor were assured the "five guarantees," which included a grain ration.[119]

Kerala. Eleven thousand government-run "Fair Price" shops keep the cost of rice and other essentials like kerosene within the reach of the poor. This subsidy accounts for as much as one-half of the total income of Kerala's poorer families.[120] Three-quarters of all school children — and most attend school — receive free meals daily.

Sri Lanka. From the postwar period to 1978, the Sri Lankan government supported the consumption of basic foods, notably rice, through a combination of free food, rationed food, and subsidized prices.[121] Since the late 1970s, however, this elaborate food security system has begun to be dismantled.[122]

Cuba. Rationing staple foods and setting price ceilings on them has kept basic food affordable and available to the Cuban people for nearly twenty-five years.[123] Under Cuba's rationing system, all citizens are guaranteed enough rice, beans, oil, sugar, meat, and other food to provide them with 1,900 calories a day.[124]

Burma we do not discuss here because its demographic data are considered unreliable and little research exists on the reasons for its slowing growth rate. We take up Colombia and Chile below, following a more detailed look at Kerala and China.

Kerala. Of these seven societies the most intriguing demographic case study — highlighting the several intertwined questions raised in this report — is that of Kerala state in India. Its population density is three times the average for all India,[125] yet commonly used indicators of hunger and poverty — infant mortality, life expectancy, and death rate — are all considerably better in Kerala than in most low-income countries as well as in India as a whole. Its infant mortality is less than one-third the national average.[126]

Other measures of welfare also reveal the relatively better position of the poor in Kerala. Besides the grain distribution system mentioned above, social security payments, pension and unemployment benefits transfer resources to the poorest groups. Expenditures on public health in Kerala, critical to any effort to reduce fertility, have historically been high. Health facilities are spread evenly throughout the state, not concentrated in the capital as in most third world countries. While land reform left significant inequality in land ownership, it did abolish tenancy, providing greater security to many who before were only renters.

These are all descriptive measures of what makes Kerala so different. But why Kerala? From the 1950s onward, political organization among the poor led to their greater self-confidence. The poor came to see health care as their right, not a gift bestowed upon them. An Indian researcher noted how this affected the delivery of health services:

> In Kerala, if a Public Health Center were unmanned for a few days, there would be a massive demonstration... [where people] would demand to be given what they knew they were entitled to.[127]

And among agricultural workers, grassroots political organization has also been the key to making land reform meaningful, to keeping wages relatively high, and to securing old-age pensions. Demographer John Caldwell notes that Kerala is one of the two societies in all of Asia where one finds the greatest grassroots determination and mobilization to secure such rights. The other is Sri Lanka—also among our list of countries exceptionally successful in reducing birth rates.[128]

Centrally important to the thesis being tested here, women's status and power in Kerala are greatly enhanced compared to other Indian states. The female literacy rate in Kerala is two-and-a-half times the all-India average.

With these few facts about life in Kerala, we can begin to understand how one of a poor country's poorest states could have achieved a population growth rate not much higher than Australia's.[129]

China. While more complex, China's recent demographic history is equally telling. From 1969 to 1979, China achieved a dramatic transition from high to low rates of fertility. Since China's population is one-fifth of the world's total and its birth rate has fallen even more rapidly than its death rate, China accounts for virtually all of the decrease in global rates of population growth in the past two decades. How was this accomplished?

Those who focus narrowly on family planning as the answer to high rates of population growth credit China's success to its aggressive family planning programs that began in the late 1960s. Through a network of "barefoot doctors" in the countryside, family planning programs reached into every village. They relied not only on making birth control freely available—including the newly developed pill—but group persuasion to change attitudes toward childbearing and family size.

Unarguably, such a concerted effort helps explain the dramatic fall in China's fertility rate in the 1970s. But viewed from the power-structures perspective, one must probe deeper. How was it possible that such a far-reaching program—unique in the world—was conceived and implemented in the first place?

China's family planning program did not arise out of thin air. It reflected prior, massive political change bringing a government to power whose ideological orientation was toward advancement for the *whole* society, not merely the narrow elite to whom the former government, as most governments, feel themselves accountable. We can unequivocally condemn China's totalitarian features while also recognizing that such a shift in power, from leadership long ignoring the needs of the Chinese peasantry to one attempting to address these needs, was a prerequisite to China's population success record. Indeed, its extensive rural health care system—a precondition for its family planning effort—would have been inconceivable without profound prior political change.

Changes in Chinese society also allowed people to respond to the family planning initiatives. Far-reaching redistribution of access to land and food, along with an assurance of old-age security, allowed the Chinese people to opt for fewer children. China's family planning motivators stressed birth planning as a way to increase prosperity for all, and, as researcher John Ratcliffe puts it, the "clearly visible redistribution of economic resources and increased opportunities for women," made that link believable.[130] Note that virtually all of China's dramatic drop in fertility occurred before 1979, that is, before implementation of its notorious one-child policy.

It was in 1979 that China's family planning policies took a new tack. Despite the dramatic success in lowering fertility, the Deng Xiaoping government believed that population growth was still hindering modernization. It instituted the world's most restrictive family planning program. Material incentives and penalties began to be offered to encourage all parents to bear only one offspring. According to Ratcliffe, "Enormous pressure—social and official—

is brought to bear on those who become 'unofficially' pregnant; few are able to resist such constant, heavy pressure, and most accede to having an abortion. While coercion is not officially sanctioned, this approach results in essentially the same outcome."[131]

At the same time, China's post-1979 approach to economic development began to undercut both guaranteed employment, and old age and medical security. Whereas in 1978, close to 90 percent of rural people were covered by a collective medical system, by 1984 less than half were included.[132] In agriculture, the "individual responsibility" system replaced collective production; private entrepreneurialism is now encouraged. The erosion of social security and widening income disparities have important consequences for fertility.

Thrown back on their own family's resources, many Chinese again see having many children — especially boys — as beneficial, both as a substitute for lost public protections and as a means of taking maximum advantage of the new economic system.[133]

In part as a result of these changes, China may be defeating its own population goals. China's birth rates have *risen* since 1980.[134]

We're not suggesting that these economic and social changes are the sole reasons for the rise. Demographer Ansley Coale of Princeton University believes that another explanation is the Chinese government's 1980 decision to relax its stringent policy governing age at marriage. And recently, enforcement of the one-child policy has been relaxed somewhat. But whatever the future of state population policies, surely these underlying economic and social changes add to pressure for higher fertility.

Chile. Until 1973, Chileans could proudly claim to live in the oldest political democracy in Latin America. From that system arose one of the most extensive public health and social security programs in the region — the key to explaining Chile's exceptional decline in population growth. Not only did these social protections contribute to an early and swift decline in infant death rates, commonly viewed as a prerequisite for reduced fertility, but they also improved the financial security of the entire population, particularly in old age. Under Chile's public health system, free or subsidized medical care, including pre-and postnatal care as well as contraceptive supplies, is made widely available through public clinics.[135]

Other factors, which are not so positive, also appear to have been at work in Chile's fertility reduction, at least in recent years. First was the tremendous social upheaval of the 1970–1973 period, when the democratically elected government of Salvador Allende was destabilized and ultimately overthrown by rightist forces aided by the U.S. government. Since then the economic policies followed by the military junta led by General Augusto Pinochet have led to such economic hardship and dislocation for the Chilean working class that having children has become increasingly unaffordable.[136] (See our earlier discussion of the role of children among the employed and unemployed poor in urban settings.)

Colombia. Of these seven societies, Colombia, not known for its government interventions on behalf of the poor, appears to defy the preconditions of security and opportunity. But not entirely. Colombia's health service sends medical interns to the countryside for one year's free service, unlike many third world countries, where medical services barely reach outside the capital city. Colombia's infant mortality is well below most lower-middle-income countries. It has also achieved high literacy rates, and an unusually high percentage of girls attend secondary school. According to the World Bank, over half of all Colombian women aged fifteen to forty-nine were at some point enrolled in primary school — even more than the comparable proportion for men (45 percent)![137]

Colombia's record also demonstrates that shifting resources toward *women*, expanding their opportunities and particularly their education, has a much bigger impact on lowering birth rates than an overall rise in income — a general pattern, according to Yale University's T. Paul Schultz.[138] Colombia's women appear to be achieving greater economic independence from men and therefore are becoming better able to determine their own fertility. They are entering the paid work force at a rapid pace.[139] Income from the coffee boom of the 1970s reportedly contributed to new economic independence for many rural women.[140]

Other Telling Examples

Thailand. Here is another country that has come very close to the achievement of those discussed above. Between 1960 and 1985, Thailand's total fertility rate fell by 50 percent; its population growth rate is currently 2.1 percent a year.[141] What factors have contributed to this decline?

The changing status of Thai women appears significant. Proportionately more women work outside the home than in other third world countries.[142] Education and wealth have been replacing motherhood and matrilineage as status markers for women, according to the University of Washington's Majorie Muecke.[143] At the same time, as education has become a societal norm, the cost of raising and educating children has risen substantially, reducing their potential economic contribution to the family.[144]

Negative changes in Thailand have also no doubt affected people's reproductive behavior. A shift from peasant to commercial agriculture, encouraged by Thailand's integration into the world market, has increased landlessness and indebtedness in the countryside. The result is greater financial insecurity for many rural Thais.[145]

Throughout our report we have linked insecurity with pressures keeping fertility high, but in Thailand (and now in Chile, too) a worsening situation appears to be contributing to fewer births, or at least not preventing the decline. An extensive government family planning program no doubt plays a part. It has made contraceptives free and easily available in rural and urban areas alike. But other aspects of Thai life must also contribute to this different reaction to economic distress. The elevated position of women, compared to most third world countries, suggests that they may have greater autonomy in making reproductive decisions.

Costa Rica. While Costa Rica has not reduced its overall population growth rate as much as the other countries highlighted here, including Thailand,[146] its fertility rates have declined a striking 53 percent between 1960 and 1985. It has managed to achieve this drop with what demographers call a weak "family planning program effort." [147] Yet the proportion of Costa Rican women using contraception is extremely high — 66 percent, or three times the rate for the rest of Central America.[148]

Why are so many Costa Rican women practicing birth control, without the strong urging of the state? The answer again seems to lie in Costa Rica's social structures, which have generated more democratic, responsive governments that have long promoted the health and education of the entire population. Costa Rica's health service is free and universal, and since the 1970s, has extended out to even the most remote rural areas. As John Caldwell describes it,

> Costa Ricans were already sufficiently well educated and egalitarian for these [health] facilities to be used fully as soon as they were provided; there was by the 1970s little need for a political revolution to teach them their rights, for that learning process had been underway for decades.[149]

Social security legislation and liberal labor codes were also introduced early on in Costa Rica, with government expenditures on social welfare getting a strong boost in the 1950s.[150] Moreover, most of Costa Rica's social welfare programs are funded by various taxes on employers, making its tax system one of the most progressive in Latin America.

Page 64

The experience of Costa Rica brings up the issue of income distribution more generally, an important measure of how power is shared in any society. Where income is highly skewed, many are cut out of participation in the economy altogether and left jobless and landless. Thus our analysis predicts that those societies with highly unequal distributions of income will typically have higher fertility as well, and vice versa. So it is not surprising to us that in several of the societies exceptionally successful in reducing growth rates, income distribution is less skewed than in the rest of the world. The distribution of household income in Sri Lanka, for example, is more equitable than in India or the United States.[151] Colombia is one of the few Latin American countries in which income distribution has actually become more equal over the last several decades.[152]

An empirical investigation also suggests a positive link between fertility decline and increased income equity. While one might question the possibility of such neat precision, one World Bank study of sixty-four different countries indicated that when the poorest groups' income goes up by one percentage point, the general fertility rate drops by almost three.[153] Adding literacy and life expectancy to the income analysis, these three factors explained 80 percent of the variation in fertility among these countries.[154] Higher literacy rates and longer life spans suggest societywide change toward greater opportunity and security.

FIVE

REFLECTIONS AND IMPLICATIONS FOR ACTION

Adding the Missing Piece to the Population Puzzle

The varied and complex histories of the societies highlighted here offer powerful lessons for all those trying to piece together the population puzzle.

They bear out our essential thesis that the population puzzle is impossible to solve without employing the concept of social power. Earlier we suggested that continued high fertility and growth reflect undemocratic power structures that deny people essential human rights. "Democratic" we defined as more than a political concept, for it applies in social, economic, and cultural life as well. Democracy can be seen as a measure of the distribution of power, existing to the degree that those affected have the power to participate in decisions or, minimally, to have their interests considered.

As the demographically successful societies we have just discussed demonstrate, the concept of power can most usefully be applied *within* societies, rather than *to* societies. The very great diversity of these societies underlines our earlier point that power is not a monolithic concept, moving uniformly through the many sectors and levels of a society. It is diverse, characterized by uneven development.

We have suggested that within each of these societies, shifts in power relations in key aspects of family, community, and national life have made lowered fertility possible: the enhanced power of women — through basic literacy, education, and employment; the heightened power of peasants to provide food and income for themselves because reforms have widely dispersed access to land; the bolstered power of consumers to secure adequate nutrition where deliberate policies have been implemented to keep basic food staples within the reach of all; the enhanced capacity of people to protect their health as medical care is accessible for the first time; and the heightened power of women to limit their births through birth control. These are some vital measures of changes needed for people to be able to choose fewer children.

In sum, convincing historical evidence suggests that when individuals and families are gaining power because their rights are protected — particularly the rights to education, medical care including contraception, old-age security, and access to income-producing resources — they no longer have to depend only on their own families for survival. Understandably, without such change, choosing smaller families remains beyond people's reach.

A Country's Poverty Is No Excuse

A final point deserves attention before broadening our vision to build on the implications of this report.

Earlier we quoted those who suggest that many third world countries are just too poor to address rapid population growth through economic and social development, so they must take the bargain route: family planning. Surely the examples given here demonstrate the fallacy of this easy out. Of the seven societies cited for their exceptionally rapid drop in fertility and population growth, four are among the world's poorest: China, Sri Lanka, Burma, and the Indian state of Kerala. The political, economic, and cultural changes that allowed population growth to slow dramatically did not depend upon first achieving high per capita income. Poverty is therefore no excuse for the continuing violation of basic human rights to essential resources.

Broadening the Vision

We believe that the power-structures perspective outlined in this report has much to offer, but we are also aware of potential pitfalls in its conceptualization and application. Stressing that it is the relationships among people that lie at the root of the interrelated problems of hunger, poverty, and rapid population growth, those taking this perspective—including ourselves at the Institute for Food and Development Policy—easily risk being misunderstood. We can be heard to say that humanity faces no resource limitation—that as long as people have enough to eat, the nation (or the world) cannot be considered overpopulated.

On a deeper level, the very fact that the power-structures analysis focuses on *human* rights may lead some to assume that it is blind to humanity's wider moral obligations. It might appear to reinforce, or at least fail to take us beyond, a human-centered lack of concern for nonhuman members of the community of all living beings.

These could be serious shortcomings; we see them rather as valuable challenges to strengthen the power-structures perspective.

First, a power-structures perspective need not make actual or potential resource availability the test of overpopulation. Since the 1960s, those operating from the people-versus-resources perspective have linked the specter of famine to overpopulation, and in challenging this view, structural analysts have understandably focused on food, too. They have documented clearly that hunger is not caused by inadequate resources. (Our earlier works, *Food First: Beyond the Myth of Scarcity* and *World Hunger: Twelve Myths*, are examples of this documentation.)[155] Those using the power-structures perspective must now clarify that although hunger is not caused by too many people, for many other reasons one might well judge a nation to have too many people.

Even focusing strictly on human development, surely more than adequate nutrition is necessary to ensure the quality of life. Japan's 123 million people live in a land area the size of California. Bangladesh has over 100 million in an area the size of Wisconsin. Even though both have the capacity to feed themselves — Japan through imports and Bangladesh by developing its own agricultural potential — might not these countries be considered overpopulated on any number of criteria?

To thrive, human beings need a pollution-free environment to protect health and enough physical space to allow for intellectual and spiritual growth. And certainly, human well-being, in the eyes of many, is enhanced by the opportunity merely to enjoy an environment undefaced and untransformed by human manipulation. In attempting to show that hunger does not result from per capita resource limits, the power-structuralist need not lose sight of these important values. The power-structures perspective emphasizes the quality of human relations and can well be broadened to include the quality of our lives within the larger natural world we inhabit.

This analysis can therefore serve all those concerned about the quality of life for yet unborn generations and their need for resources. At the same time, it can incorporate the insights of environmental philosophers, ecologists, ethicists, and religiously attuned people who are now challenging humanity's assumption that if *people* are thriving, then everything is all right. The accelerating destruction of irreplaceable rain forests, the historically unprecedented obliteration of species, the erosion of plant genetic diversity, and the depletion of the earth's protective ozone layer represent a moral crisis beyond humanity's well-being alone. Many people are coming to realize that the infinitely rich biosphere itself must be considered of innate worth.[156]

In other words, the power-structures analysis need not imply that solutions lie simply in making fairer and more democratic access to the fruits of a narrowly human-centered economic development model. The analysis can show how the same antidemocratic structures keeping fertility high also play a central role in environmental destruction. But it can go still further — incorporating insights of those questioning *any* model of development that perceives the environment merely as a pool of resources for human use.

Effective Responses to the Population Problem

Now, decades after the population explosion first went off and with considerable experience in trying to defuse it, we must look unflinchingly at the lessons to be learned. The realization that the population explosion is a complex social fact is not enough; we will have to do more than pay lip service to its social roots if we are serious about meeting the crisis.

To continue to focus narrowly on birth control strategies is to imply that regardless of what we know about the real roots of the problem, better birth control is all we in the industrial West can offer. We do not accept this view, especially as U.S citizens. As a major world power, the United States government directly and indirectly shapes the behavior of many foreign governments. It is inconceivable that the United States would ever stop using its foreign policy to aid those governments it deems supportive of its own interests. Thus it is by becoming citizen activists that Americans who are troubled by the dire consequences of high population growth rates can make their most effective contribution.

Working to change our own government's perception of the kind of foreign governments it can support may be the single most important way American citizens can help address the population problem. Until our government transcends its deep fear of redistributive change abroad, our tax dollars will continue to go to support governments blocking the very changes we outline in this report, those necessary to allow people the option of smaller families.

U.S. policy toward the Philippines illustrates this point. The population growth rate in the Philippines is among the highest in Southeast Asia, while its people are among the poorest and hungriest. Seventy percent of the rural people either lack land altogether or lack secure tenure to the land they farm; and they must turn over much of what they produce to absentee landowners. The United States supplied billions of dollars to maintain the former martial law government of Ferdinand Marcos, which not only refused to reform this gross imbalance in access to resources, but furthered economic concentration. Since 1986, the Philippines has had a new government, but one still unwilling to seriously confront the underlying insecurity at the root of hunger and high birth rates. It, too, receives enormous U.S. military, economic, and diplomatic support.

Ever since the Philippines was a colony of the United States, our government has played a central role in shaping that country's domestic policy. But the emphasis of that attention has been on military buildup to defeat internal uprising and on economic development favorable to the interests of wealthy Filipinos and U.S. investors. Never has the United States made its economic and political support conditional on domestic policies addressing the undemocratic economic structures that stand in the way of a significant drop in birth rates.

Such a change cannot come about until U.S. citizens reorient their government's understanding of what is in our own interests. For detailed support for this position, see our previous work *Betraying the National Interest*.[157] There we argue that maintaining structures denying majorities the essentials for survival and dignity is not serving U.S. interests. The same argument can be made about U.S. policies toward Central American countries, which have among the highest birth rates in the world. Simply funding a family planning initiative in the Philippines or in Honduras, for example, is woefully inadequate. U.S. citizens must be willing to do something much more controversial: explicitly identify the link between U.S. policies and the very reasons why birth rates are high to begin with and use one's voice as a citizen to alter those ties.

Taking population seriously means incorporating the concept of power as an indispensable tool of analysis and facing the logical consequences. It means learning from the clear historical evidence. Without more democratic structures of decision making power, from the family to the global arena, there is no solution — short of dehumanizing coercion — to the population explosion.

Because we have no time to waste with approaches that cannot work, we must face the evidence telling us that the fate of the world — whether it becomes miserably overcrowded — hinges on the fate of today's poor majorities. Only as they are empowered to achieve greater security and opportunity can population growth halt.

NOTES

1. Michael S. Teitelbaum, "Relevance of Demographic Transition Theory for Developing Countries," *Science* 188 (2 May 1975): 420–425.

2. UN Fund for Population Activities, *1986 Annual Report* (New York: UNFPA, 1986), 7.

3. Personal communication, January 1988. Cutright is with the Department of Sociology, Indiana University, Bloomington.

4. News Release from the Population Reference Bureau, 28 April 1988.

5. Julian Simon, "Resources, Population, Environment: An Oversupply of False Bad News," *Science* 208 (27 June 1980): 1434. According to Simon, productivity will be raised not only through economies of scale and larger markets, but also through the addition of more people's contributions to knowledge and technical progress. See also Julian Simon, *The Ultimate Resource* (Princeton, New Jersey: Princeton University Press, 1981).

6. Simon, "Resources, Population, Environment," 1434.

7. National Academy of Sciences, Working Group on Population Growth and Economic Development, *Population Growth and Economic Development: Policy Questions* (Washington: National Academy Press, 1986), 17.

8. Paul Ehrlich, *The Population Bomb* (New York: Ballantine Books, 1968), prologue.

9. William and Paul Paddock, *Famine 1975!* (Boston: Little, Brown and Co., 1967; renamed *Time of Famines*, 1976).

10. Lester R. Brown and Jodi L. Jacobson, "Our Demographically Divided World," Worldwatch Paper no. 74 (Washington: Worldwatch Institute, December 1986), 5.

11. Ibid.

12. Garrett Hardin, "Living on a Lifeboat," *BioScience* 24 (October 1974): 561–568.

13. View expressed in televised debate with Frances Moore Lappé, July 1987.

14. Per capita cropland from Francis Urban and Thomas Vollrath, *Patterns and Trends in World Agricultural Land Use,* U.S. Department of Agriculture, Economic Research Service, Foreign Agricultural Economic Report no. 198, Washington, D.C., 1984, table 2, 1984. Life expectancy from World Bank, *World Development Report 1985* (New York: Oxford University Press, 1985), table 1, 174. According to the Kissinger Commission report, officially the *Report of the National Bipartisan Commission on Central America,* Washington, D.C., 1984, "57 percent of Honduras' families live in extreme poverty, unable to pay the cost of the basic basket of food."

15. "Children: A Cost to the Rich, A Benefit to the Poor," *The New Internationalist* (June 1977): 16-17, cited in Morley and Lovel, *My Name Is Today,* 34. For more detail on this particular study, see *Population and Development Review,* September 1977.

16. M. T. Cain, "The Economic Activities of Children in a Village in Bangladesh," *Population and Development Review* 3 (1977): 201–228, cited in W. Murdoch, *The Poverty of Nations,* (Baltimore: Johns Hopkins University Press, 1980), 26.

17. C. Lwechungura Kamuzora, "High Fertility and the Demand for Labor in Peasant Economies: The Case of Bukoba District, Tanzania," *Development and Change* 15, no. 1 (January 1984): 105–123.

18. "Hundred Dollar Slaves," *The New Internationalist* (October 1986): 9.

19. John C. Caldwell, *Theory of Fertility Decline* (New York: Academic Press, 1982), 37, cited in Betsy Hartmann, *Reproductive Rights and Wrongs* (New York: Harper and Row, 1987), 7.

20. John Caldwell, *Theory of Fertility Decline,* 69.

21. M. Nag, B. White, and R. C. Peet, "An Anthropological Approach to the Study of the Economic Value of Children in Java and Nepal," *Current Anthropology* 19 (1978): 293–306.

22. World Bank, *The World Development Report 1984* (New York: Oxford University Press, 1984), 52.

23. Mead Cain, "Fertility as an Adjustment to Risk," *Population and Development Review* 9, no. 4 (December 1983): 688–701, especially 699.

24. A recent study of Thailand, for instance, found that large families are increasingly perceived as an economic burden in part because the cost of educating children has risen substantially. See Knodel et al., "Fertility

Transition in Thailand: A Qualitative Analysis," *Population and Development Review* 10, no. 2 (June 1984): 297–328.

25. Thomas Merrick, "Recent Fertility Declines in Brazil, Colombia, and Mexico," World Bank Staff Working Paper no. 692 (Washington D.C.: World Bank, 1985).

26. India's Sixth Five Year Plan, 374, cited in Sheila Zurbrigg, *Rakku's Story: Studies of Ill-Health and the Source of Change* (Madras: George Joseph Printing Company, 1984), 70.

27. Interview with two women doctors on family planning, *Connexions*, Summer/Fall 1985, 49.

28. Murdoch, *Poverty of Nations*, 45.

29. Perdita Huston, *Message from the Village* (New York: The Epoch B Foundation, 1978), 119, cited in Hartmann, *Reproductive Rights and Wrongs*, 48.

30. Jodi L. Jacobson, "Planning the Global Family," Worldwatch Paper no. 80, Washington D.C., Worldwatch Institute, December 1987, 20.

31. Ibid., 21.

32. Faruqee and Gulhati, *Rapid Population Growth in Sub-Saharan Africa, Issues and Policies*, World Bank Staff Working Paper no. 559, Washington D.C., World Bank, 1983, 48–52.

33. Ibid., 54.

34. Sally Mugabe, "High Fertility Hampers Women's Status," *Popline* (June 1987): 2. *Popline* is a publication of the World Population News Service.

35. Medea Benjamin, ed., *Don't Be Afraid, Gringo: A Honduran Woman Speaks from the Heart* (Food First Books, 1987), 47.

36. Huston, *Message from the Village*, 38.

37. Hartmann, *Reproductive Rights and Wrongs*, 247–248.

38. Charlene Spretnak in "The Population Bomb: An Explosive Issue for the Environmental Movement," *Utne Reader* (May/June 1988): 86–87.

39. World Resources Institute, *World Resources 1986* (New York: Basic Books, 1986), 21.

40. Betsy Hartmann, personal correspondence, January 1988.

41. Hartmann's *Reproductive Rights and Wrongs*, as well as chapter 3 of our own Institute's book, *World Hunger: Twelve Myths*, are only two of the most recent expressions of this attempt to incorporate a gender-based analysis of power within a larger structural framework.

42. Susan George, "Debt: The Profit of Doom," *Food First Action Alert*, Institute for Food and Development Policy, San Francisco, 1988. See also George, *Fate Worse than Debt* (New York: Grove Press/Food First Books, 1988).

43. Ralph R. Sell and Steven J. Kunitz, "The Debt Crisis and the End of an Era in Mortality Decline," *Studies in Comparative International Development*, 1987, cited in George, *Fate Worse than Debt*, 134.

44. Alan Riding, "In Northeastern Brazil Poverty Cycle Goes On," *New York Times*, 3 May 1988, A4.

45. Kevin Danaher, Phillip Berryman, Medea Benjamin, "Help or Hindrance: United States Economic Aid in Central America," *Food First Development Report* no. 1, September 1987, 19–21.

46. Personal communication, 31 December 1987.

47. Mary Kay Magistrad, "Family Planning Program Under Fire in Bangladesh," *Christian Science Monitor*, 2 June 1988, 11.

48. Jodi L. Jacobson, "Planning the Global Family," 5.

49. Ibid., 5–6.

50. Ibid., 45.

51. Ibid., 13.

52. Judith Jacobsen, "Promoting Population Stabiliization: Incentives for Small Families," Worldwatch Paper no. 54, Worldwatch Institute, Washington, D.C., June 1983, 8.

53. During this period, an estimated 83 percent of all contraceptive users were sterilized (see Jacobson, "Planning the Global Family," 41).

54. J. S. Satia and Rushikesh M. Maru, "Incentives and Disincentives in the Indian Family Welfare Program," *Studies in Family Planning* 17, no. 3 (May/June 1986): 142.

55. Hartmann, *Reproductive Rights*, 237–8.

56. Hartmann, personal correspondence; also see *New York Times*, 11

January 1988, 4.

57. Satia and Maru, "Incentives and Disincentives," 136–145.

58. Interview with an Indian researcher who wishes to remain anonymous, August 1987.

59. Ibid., 138.

60. Betsy Hartmann, personal correspondence. Note also that women tend to earn less than the average, and few Bangladeshis have steady employment at any wage.

61. Hartmann, *Reproductive Rights*, 214.

62. Ibid., 218.

63. Ibid., 216.

64. Betsy Hartmann, *Food, Saris and Sterilization: Population Control in Bangladesh* (London: Bangladesh International Action Group, 1985), 17.

65. More specifically, the Community-Based Integrated Rural Development program, as it's called, offers loans, direct credit, and farm inputs to rural families. See John Stoeckel et al., "Maintaining Family Planning Acceptance Levels through Development Incentives in Northeastern Thailand," *Studies in Family Planning* 17, no. 1 (January/February 1986): 36–43.

66. S. Surjaningrat and R. H. Pardoko, "Review of Some of the Management Aspects of the Indonesian Population and Family Planning Programme," Technical Report Series of the National Family Planning Coordination Board, Monograph no. 37, Indonesia, 1983, 3.

67. World Bank, *World Development Report 1984*, 125.

68. Linda Atkinson et al., "Prospects for Improved Contraception," *Family Planning Perspectives*, July/August, 1980, cited in Jacobson, "Planning the Global Family," 30.

69. Ibid., 30–31.

70. Despite the fact that the Food and Drug Administration has not approved its use, several articles in the *New York Times* recently reported that Depo-provera is being administered as a contraceptive by the Indian Health Service. Although only 35 Native American women are currently being given the drug, at least 200 were prescribed it in the past. See

"Indian Agency Using a Banned Contraceptive," *New York Times*, 7 August 1987, 8; and "Depo Provera and the Indian Women," Editorial, *New York Times*, 17 August 1987, 18.

71. Lynn Duggan, "From Birth Control to Population Control," *Southeast Asia Chronicle* 96 (January 1985): 28–31.

72. Duggan, "From Birth Control," 28–29; Linda Golley, "Health Care in Southeast Asia," *Southeast Asia Chronicle*, (June 1982): 7.

73. Duggan, "From Birth Control," 29; Also see World Health Organization, *Injectable Hormonal Contraceptives: Technical Aspects and Safety* (Geneva: World Health Organization, 1982), 17–23.

74. WHO Collaborative Study of Neoplasia and Steroid Contraceptives, "Invasive Cervical Cancer and Depot-medroxyprogesterone Acetate," *Bulletin of the World Health Organization* 63, no. 3 (1985): 508; L. C. Powell and R. J. Seymour, "Effects of Depot-medroxyprogesterone Acetate as a Contraceptive Agent," *American Journal of Obstetrics and Gynecology* 110 (1971): 36–41. Another preliminary study by the WHO Collaborative Group suggests that Depo-provera is not linked to increased risk of breast cancer, as originally suspected (WHO Collaborative Study of Neoplasia and Steroid Contraceptives, "Breast Cancer and Depot-medroxyprogesterone Acetate," *Bulletin of the World Health Organization*. 63, no. 3 (1985): 513–519).

75. Duggan, "From Birth Control," 29.

76. Ibid.

77. UN Economic and Social Council, cited in Caroline Pratt, "Whose Right To Choose? State Control of Fertility in South Africa and Namibia" (Master's thesis, University of Wisconsin, 1988).

78. Pratt, "Whose Right To Choose?," 21, citing a number of studies and reports.

79. Jacobson, "Planning the Global Family," 31.

80. Ibid.; see also Hartmann, *Reproductive Rights, 196.*

81. Jacobson, "Planning the Global Family," 31.

82. Hartmann, *Reproductive Rights*, 197.

83. These include disruption of the menstrual cycle, headache, depression, loss of sex drive, weight change, nausea, and acne. Norplant is also

not recommended for lactating women. See Ibid., 197.

84. Firman Lubis et al., "One Year Experience with NORPLANT Implants in Indonesia," Studies in Family Planning, 14 (June/July 1983): 183.

85. Satia and Maru, "Incentives and Disincentives," 145-46.

86. The proportion of married Mexican women who were sterilized in 1976 was 7 percent; by 1982, it had risen to 29 percent. (During the same period, the use of all other methods fell.) Note that these figures refer to married women using contraception, not to all women. See Francisco Alba and Joseph Potter, "Population and Development in Mexico Since 1940: An Interpretation," Population and Development Review 12, no. 1 (March 1986), table 5.

87. Alba and Potter, "Population and Development in Mexico," table 5.

88. Lincoln Bergman et al., Puerto Rico: The Flame of Resistance (San Francisco: People's Press, 1977), 117. It should be noted, however, that the government did not establish an official sterilization program until 1974; when it did, the program came under the jurisdiction of the Division of Family Planning in the Department of Health. See Harriet B. Presser, "Puerto Rico: Recent Trends in Fertility and Sterilization," International Family Planning Perspectives 6 (March 1980): 20–25.

89. Bergman et al, Puerto Rico: The Flame of Resistance, 118.

90. Presser, "Puerto Rico: Recent Trends," 20.

91. Ibid., 22.

92. Hartmann, Reproductive Rights, 232.

93. Ana Maria Garcia, La Operacion (film), 1980.

94. Magistrad, "Family Planning Program Under Fire in Bangladesh."

95. Benjamin, ed., Don't Be Afraid Gringo, 48–9.

96. Phillips Cutright, "Family Planning Programs or Development: The Debate Continues," International Family Planning Perspectives 12, no. 3 (September 1986): 105.

97. W. Parker Mauldin, Bernard Berelson, and Zenas Sykes, "Conditions of Fertility Decline in Developing Countries, 1965–1975," Studies in Family Planning 9, no. 5 (May 1978): 121. See also, Robert J. Lapham and

W. P. Mauldin, "Contraceptive Prevalence: The Influence of Organized Family Planning Programs," *Studies in Family Planning* 16, no. 3 (May–June 1985) for a more updated, though slightly different, analysis.

98. Lapham and Mauldin, "Contraceptive Prevalence," 124.

99. It is in Kerala that India's first "family planning camps," criticized as extremely coercive, were held in 1970 and 1971. See J. K. Satia and Rushikesh M. Maru, "Incentives and Disincentives in the Indian Family Welfare Program," *Studies in Family Planning* 17, no. 3 (May/June 1986): 136–145. Our point, however, is that this effort did not "take" until social conditions were right.

100. K. C. Zachariah, "The Anomaly of the Fertility Decline in India's Kerala State," World Bank Staff Working Paper no. 700 (Washington D.C.: World Bank, 1984), 6.

101. Rates of change in Indian fertility were calculated using data provided by Bruce Fuller of the World Bank's Population Division.

102. News Release of the Population Reference Bureau, 28 April 1988.

103. Data provided by Bruce Fuller of the World Bank's Population Division.

104. Hector L. Dieguez, "Social Consequences of the Economic Crisis: Mexico" (Unpublished paper by the World Bank, Washington, 1986), 4.

105. See, for instance Francisco Alba and Joseph Potter, "Population and Development in Mexico Since 1940: An Interpretation," *Population and Development Review* 12, no. 1 (March 1986), especially table 4.

106. In the "Social Consequences of the Economic Decline: Mexico," Dieguez refers to a 1983 survey done by Mexico's National Consumer Institute, which shows a significant decline in the consumption of oil, meat, sugar, eggs, beans, fruits, legumes, milk, bread, and fish. Not surprisingly, these declines were concentrated among the poorest households.

107. The Thai-American Project, "The Role of the State in the Problem of Malnutrition Among the Children of Thailand" (Unpublished paper, Santa Monica, California, February 1986), 2.

108. The Thai-American Project, "The Role of the State," 1.

109. *FAO Trade Yearbook 1983* (Rome: Food and Agriculture Organization, 1984), tables 10, 41, 48, 66, and 175.

110. Kraisak Choonhavan et al., United Nations Institute for Training and Research, Thailand Country Report, prepared for the UNITAR International Conference on "Alternative Development Strategies and the Future of Asia," New Delhi, 11–17 March 1980, 24.

111. The total fertility rate for India is now about 4.5 children per woman. The 25-year period referred to is 1960 to 1985. Data from the World Bank's Population Division.

112. U.S. Department of Agriculture, Economic Research Service, *Agricultural Outlook* (December 1985): 14–18.

113. *FAO Trade Yearbook 1985* (Rome: Food and Agriculture Organization, 1986), 39, table 169.

114. World Bank, *World Development Report 1987*, table 27. Note that we've included Cuba in this list of 74 low and lower-middle income countries because it was so classified for the first period of our time series. Only in recent years has the World Bank reclassified Cuba as a "nonreporting nonmember economy." Also note that countries of a million or less in population are excluded from the bank's statistics.

115. Statistically, two other countries might be included in this group: El Salvador and Mauritius. The first we exclude because its slow growth results from out migration and disruption and death from war. The second, an island whose population only recently passed a million, is so dissimilar to the other countries as to make meaningful comparisons impossible. Data on growth rates are from the World Bank's *World Development Report* (1984 and 1987) and represent averages for the 1980–85 period. Total fertility rates also come from the World Bank and were provided to us by Bruce Fuller of the bank's Population Division. We use total fertility rates instead of crude birth rates because the former should not be affected by shifts in the size of the cohort of women who are of childbearing age that could occur over a 25-year period.

116. According to the Indian Census, the population growth rate of Kerala averaged 1.8 percent annually between 1971 and 1981 (*Census of India*, Kerala State, part 2A, statements 3 and 8, pp. 28 and 32). Interview with Dr. K. C. Zachariah at the World Bank, Population and Human Resources Division, April 1986.

117. Murdoch, *Poverty of Nations*, 89.

118. Robert J. Lapham and W. Parker Mauldin, "Contraceptive Prevalance: The Influence of Organized Family Planning Programs," *Studies in Family Planning* 16 (May/June 1985): 177–137.

119. See for example: Elizabeth Croll, *The Family Rice Bowl: Food and the Domestic Economy in China* (Geneva: UN Research Institute for Social Development, 1982).

120. S. Kumar, *The Impact of Subsidized Rice on Food Consumption in Kerala*, Research Report no. 5 (Washington, D.C.: International Food Policy Research Institute, 1979).

121. U.S. Agency for International Development, *Sri Lanka: The Impact of PL 480 Title I Assistance*, AID Project Impact Evaluation Report no. 39 (Washington, D.C., October 1982), C-8.

122. Ibid., C-13. Since the 1970s, the food consumption of the lowest income groups has fallen both in quantity and in quality (less dried fish and beans).

123. Medea Benjamin, Joseph Collins, and Michael Scott, *No Free Lunch: Food and Revolution in Cuba Today* (New York: Grove Press/Food First, 1986), 26.

124. Ibid., 92. In 1983, in fact, the Organization of American States reported that Cuba ranked second in Latin America in per capita food availability.

125. A. V. Jose, "Poverty and Inequality: The Case of Kerala," in *Poverty in Rural Asia*, ed. Azizur Rahman Khan and Eddy Lee (Bangkok: International Labour Organization, Asian Employment Programme, 1983), 108.

126. *World Development Forum* 6 (29 February 1988): 1, quoting the New Delhi Family Planning Foundation. The infant mortality rate in India is 100; in Kerala it is 30. See also John Ratcliffe, "Social Justice and the Demographic Transition: Lessons from India's Kerala State," in *Practicing Health for All*, ed. D. Morley, J. Rohde, and G. Williams (Oxford: Oxford University Press, 1983); Ratcliffe "Toward a Social Justice Theory of Demographic Transition: Lessons from India's Kerala State," *Janasamkhya* (Kerala University) 1 (June 1983).

127. Quoted in John Caldwell, "Routes to Low Mortality in Poor Countries," *Population and Development Review* 12 (June 1986): 198.

128. Caldwell, "Routes to Low Mortality, 191–4.

129. *World Bank Development Report*, 1987, table 27.

130. John Ratcliffe, "China's Population Policies: Attempting to Solve the Wrong Problem?" *Politique de Population*, Summer 1988, in press.

131. Ibid.

132. Ibid.

133. This may well explain the apparent rise in female infanticide in China since the 1979 change in policy. See "The Threat of Population Growth," *World Press Review* (August 1987):59.

134. Ratcliffe, "China's Population Policies." See also News Release from the Population Reference Bureau, 28 April 1988.

135. Personal communication with demography professor Alberto Palloni at the University of Wisconsin, December 1987. Another explanation of the decline in Chile's fertility offered by Dr. Palloni has to do with the strong European influence which still exists in Chile today. According to Palloni, this European influence has led to a relative openness in attitudes towards contraception.

136. Note that the Pinochet government's economic policies were originally designed and overseen by conservative U.S. economist Milton Friedman and his "Chicago boys," as they are colloquially known. For more on these policies, see Elton Rayack, *Not So Free to Choose* (New York: Praeger, 1987) and Alejandro Foxley, *Latin American Experiments in Neo-Conservative Economics* (Berkeley: University of California Press, 1983).

137. See World Bank, *World Development Report 1984*, 198–199.

138. Interview with T. Paul Schultz, an economist and population specialist at Yale University, May 1986. Studies documenting the reduction in fertility associated with women's education abound.

139. Interview with Dr. Carmen Diana Deere, Department of Economics, University of Massachusetts, January 1986, and with Sherry Keith, World Bank officer, January 1986.

140. Interview with Dr. Nola Reinhart, Department of Economics, Smith College, April 1986.

141. Thailand's population growth rate during the 1960s averaged 3.1 percent per year, implying a 27 percent decline over the last 2 decades.

142. U.S. Agency for International Development, *Women of the World: A Chartbook for Developing Regions, Asia* (Washington D.C.: Bureau of the Census, 1985) 33–34.

143. Marjorie A. Muecke, "Make Money Not Babies: Changing Status Markers of Northern Thai Women," *Asian Survey* 24, no. 4 (April 1984): 459–469. Knodel et. al make a similar point in their article "Fertility Transition in Thailand: A Qualitative Analysis" noting that aspirations for consumer goods has increased greatly in Thailand, presumably motivating a greater desire for wealth. See *Population and Development Review* 10, no. 2 (June 1984): 297–328.

144. Knodel et al., "Fertility Transition in Thailand: A Qualitative Analysis," *Population and Development Review* 10, no. 2 (June 1984): 297–328.

145. Chayan Vaddhanaphuti and Martha Winnacker, "Old Cash Structures and New Crops," *Southeast Asia Chronicle* 86 (October 1982): 3–9, esp. table 3. Also see M. Muecke, "Make Money, Not Babies"; Knodel et al., "Fertility Transition," 302; and Hartmann, *Reproductive Rights and Wrongs*, 7. It should be noted, however, that the impact of increased landlessness could just as well have the opposite effect, i.e., of stimulating fertility. While growing landlessness may lessen the need for extra farm hands, it can simultaneously increase a family's need for income earners, since more food must now be purchased.

146. The population growth rate in Costa Rica averaged 2.7 percent a year for the 1980–85 period.

147. Lapham and Mauldin, "Contraceptive Prevalence," 123, table 1.

148. The average contraceptive prevalence rate for Guatemala, El Salvador, Honduras, and Nicaragua combined is 22 percent. Also note that Costa Rica shows the highest contraceptive use of 28 countries classified as having weak family planning program efforts, and a higher rate than 16 countries with moderate family planning efforts, with the notable exception of Cuba (see Lapham and Mauldin, "Contraceptive Prevalence," 123, table 1).

149. Caldwell, "Routes to Low Mortality," 200.

150. Ibid., 199.

151. World Bank, *World Development Report 1984*, table 28, 272.

152. Miguel Urrutia, *Winners and Losers in Colombia's Economic Growth of the 1970s* (London: Oxford University Press, 1985), 86–87.

153. The study also controlled for per capita GNP differences. "The poorest groups" here refers to the bottom 40 percent of the population by income. World Bank, *Population Policies and Economic Development*, A World Bank Staff Report, Timothy King, coordinating author (Baltimore: Johns Hopkins University Press, 1974), appendix A, 147. See also Robert Repetto, *The Interaction of Fertility and the Size Distribution of Income*, Harvard Center for Population Studies, Research Papers Series no. 8, (Cambridge, Mass., October 1974).

154. World Bank, *Population Policies*, 147.

155. Frances Moore Lappé and Joseph Collins with Cary Fowler, *Food First: Beyond the Myth of Scarcity* (New York: Ballantine, 1977); Frances Moore Lappé and Joseph Collins, *World Hunger: Twelve Myths* (New York and San Francisco: Grove Press/Food First Books, 1986).

156. See, for example, Baird Callicott, *In Defense of the Land Ethic* (Albany: State University of New York Press, 1988); Holmes Ralston, III, *Philosophy Gone Wild: Essays in Environmental Ethics* (Buffalo, New York: Prometheus Press, 1986).

157. Frances Moore Lappé, Rachel Schurman, Kevin Danaher, *Betraying the National Interest* (New York and San Francisco: Grove Press/Food First Books, 1988).

SELECTED RESOURCES FROM FOOD FIRST

- ☐ *A Fate Worse Than Debt* ($8.95)
- ☐ *Betraying the National Interest* ($8.95)
- ☐ *Don't Be Afraid, Gringo* ($(.95)
- ☐ *World Hunger: Twelve Myths* ($9.95)
- ☐ *Brave New Third World: Strategies for Survival in the Global Economy* ($6)
- ☐ *The Philippines: Fire on the Rim* ($9.95)
- ☐ *Kerala: Radical Reform as Development in an Indian State* ($6)

- ☐ Please send me a free Food First Catalog
- ☐ I want to become a member of Food First. Enclosed is my tax-deductible contribution of $25 or more.

$$\begin{aligned}
\text{Amount of order (\$2 minimum)} \quad &\$\_\_\_\_ \\
\text{6.7\% sales tax (CA residents)} \quad &\$\_\_\_\_ \\
\text{15\% postage and handling (\$1 minimum)} \quad &\$\_\_\_\_ \\
\text{TOTAL} \quad &\$\_\_\_\_
\end{aligned}$$

Please charge to my ☐ Visa ☐ MC

Name on Card_____

Card No. _____Expires _____

Signature_____

NAME_____

ADDRESS_____

CITY_____STATE_____ZIP_____

FOOD FIRST BOOKS 145 Ninth Street, San Francisco, CA 94706 (415) 864-8555